£20.

Astorga

Nicaragua

NO OTHER REALITY

the life and times
of
Nora Astorga

Patricia Daniel

NO OTHER REALITY
the life and times of Nora Astorga

Copyright: Patricia Daniel

First published 1998 by CAM
c/o The Greenhouse, 1 Trevelyan Terrace, Bangor LL57 1AX

Printed by Gwasg Pantycelyn
Lôn Ddewi, Caernarfon LL55 1ER

ISBN 0 9532423 0 7

Cover photo by courtesy of Associated Press
Nora Astorga, Nicaragua's Vice-Foreign Minister,
confirmed on Tuesday March 20 (1984)
at the Sandino's International airport
that she was appointed as the new Nicaraguan ambassador
to the United States within the next four weeks
'once the US government gives the approval.'

to

Dora

and all women born or reborn in Nicaragua

Acknowledgements

Unless otherwise indicated, Nora's own comments are taken from the interview published posthumously as <u>Nora Astorga in her own words</u> or the Spanish version <u>Nora Astorga guerrillera... embajadora de la paz y de la vida</u> both from *Envio*, the monthly magazine of analysis on Nicaragua.

Thanks are due to the many people who helped me further my research and shared their memories of Nora with me through letters, interviews and conversations between the autumn of 1994 and summer 1996. I should like to mention here:

Guadelupe Salinas, José María Alvarado (Chester), Dora Zeledón, Jorgé Jenkins Molieri, Sister Rina Molina, Victor Hugo Tinoco, Carlos Tünnermann, Grethel Vargas and a nun, former teacher of Nora at the Colegio Teresiano, who prefers for religious reasons to remain anonymous.

Lea Guido was interviewed in July 1996 by Margaret Nixon and Dierdre Hyde in San José and María Cristina Najlis was interviewed in July 1996 by Margaret Nixon in Managua.

Special thanks are offered to Doña Muriel Astorga for her willingness to talk about her daughter and her kind invitation to visit the family home in Managua on two occasions.

A particular debt is owed to Margaret Randall for the initial inspiration for this book and her support for the project. I have drawn on Margaret's crucially important oral history work, which covers different aspects of the Nicaraguan revolution, to help provide the context for Nora's story.

Thanks are also due to former colleagues at the Universidad Centroamericana, Managua; to Helen Yuill and members of the UK Nicaragua Solidarity Campaign; to Katabasis for permission to reproduce some of the poems; and to Monica Lira who helped with newspaper searches in Washington. Diana Mills provided support at a crucial stage in the project and Jo Wells deserves a special mention for her selfless editing. Last but not least, thanks to Tom and Tony.

Contents

Foreword

I was in Nicaragua in 1987 and experienced the awful reality of living in a country torn apart by war. I was overwhelmed by a sense of sadness, of the damaging effects war can have upon a country, but I was also inspired by the passion and dedication of the people to their cause. My time in Nicaragua affected me in many ways and I feel honoured to have been asked to write the foreword to this inspirational book.

It is very difficult to ask an outsider to fully realise what exactly the Nicaraguans have done - not only was their county consumed by a vicious war for ten years, but along with other countries of the region they had to face the added burden of what is known as the Latin American lost decade. Nicaragua's task during this decade was to begin a very painful process of reconstruction and it is only within this framework that the situation of women in Nicaragua can be understood.

Many women saw the revolution as an awakening of their political consciousness. It taught them that they had a right to speak and that what they said was as important as any words spoken by a man. It taught them they had a right to education, health and political participation. The revolutionary spirit is today perhaps most alive in the women and their continuing struggle for recognition of their basic human rights. As in most countries, women are amongst the poorest in Nicaragua and the majority of households are headed by them.

I feel strongly that as a socialist it is my duty to support the construction of a new society, while acknowledging the problems faced in this endeavour. This book is a step towards an understanding of the problems and a recognition of women's continuing struggle.

Eluned Morgan
MEP for Mid and West Wales
March 1997

Introduction

I first went to Nicaragua in winter 1985/86 to work on the coffee harvest as a member of a brigade organised by the British Nicaragua Solidarity Campaign. Living in the mountains we learnt a great deal about the Nicaraguan revolution - how everyone had their rôle to play in defending the revolutionary process. We were thrilled by how much it was possible to achieve through sheer commitment and belief.

During my stay I was offered a teaching job at the Catholic university, the Universidad Centroamericana, in Managua. I quickly rearranged my life in London and returned to Nicaragua to take up the job. Shortly afterwards I discovered that I was pregnant and my daughter Dora was born in Managua on February 12, 1987. She has Nicaraguan nationality and because of her I have residency rights in the country.

The following year, still in Managua, we celebrated Dora's first birthday. Two days later we heard that Ambassador Nora Astorga had died. I never met her, but even before I went to Nicaragua I knew something of her earlier participation in the revolution. This was through an interview published in Margaret Randall's excellent book 'Sandino's Daughters: Testimonies of Women in Struggle.'

Nora Astorga was a student activist and political organiser, an undercover agent and then a guerrilla fighter during the 1979 insurrection against the dictator Somoza. She worked as the Public Prosecutor in charge of the trials against war criminals and later became Ambassador to the United Nations. After a brief but brilliant diplomatic career and a long fight against cancer she died on St Valentine's Day 1988, leaving four children and aged only 39. She was honoured as a 'Hero of the Nation' and remembered as both an exemplary mother and an exemplary revolutionary.

Back in Britain, I later found the time to write a book about Nicaragua. My purpose was to re-examine what Nicaragua has meant to me, to celebrate

1

the courage of the women there and, through this, to tap into the inspiration that I felt that I had lost. I rediscovered Nora's story and at first wrote it as a novel - which was very exciting. Eventually, unsure about how to proceed, I revisited Nicaragua with my daughter in the hope of enlightenment. After talking to several people who had known Nora Astorga, I decided that in this case the truth was greater than fiction and decided to write her biography instead.

This was not the easiest choice. As I worked on the project I saw Nora becoming invisible before my eyes. Despite the fact that she was well known during her lifetime and remembered in people's hearts, there was very little documentation about her - and some of that is not entirely accurate. As time goes by dates and events become blurred, a whole year of her life seems to be lost... What did the press record of her? Actually very little. Inside Nicaragua the reports are mainly about the men that she worked with. Did she deliberately keep a low profile? That certainly didn't seem to be the case in the way she operated outside the country. However, in official sources, such as United Nations documents, Nora is often not named for her work - unlike President Daniel Ortega or Foreign Minister Miguel d'Escoto, Nora is simply referred to as 'Nicaragua'.

How much will the next generation really know about this woman? Researching Nora's life brought home to me the fact that in every generation we have to re-invent models of women's destiny because the lives of women before us have been - deliberately or otherwise - obliterated. If the rate of disappearance of a woman so public can be so quick, we all have a duty to make sure that we record what women of our own generation do. It was precisely because the search for definite information was so difficult that I strengthened my resolve to complete the task. I learnt that other people had tried to document Nora's life and had given up. I persevered because in the end I saw it as my *trinchera* (the trench in which I fought) in order to defend a part of the revolution. In another sense, I did it for my daughter, so that she will have evidence of what I have done.

I interviewed members of Nora's family, friends and colleagues in order to be able to paint a fuller picture. Some people were reluctant to speak to me - they didn't known her well enough, or they had been too close to her. Most were generous with their time and their memories. But there were problems here too - the accuracy and selectivity of memory. There is also always a risk of being told what people think you want to hear, or what you ought to believe, in other words receiving the rhetoric rather than the reality, myths repeated from newspapers or oral history. Some of the people who may have remembered more died earlier than Nora did. And even the memory of those who were close to her had begun to fade. Interestingly, men often found it easier to provide sketches, scenes of events or to recall the words that someone spoke.

Remembering Nora was an emotional experience for many people that I spoke to, not only talking about her as a daughter, friend or lover, but also talking about the revolution - the ideals and struggles that they had shared. Now living under a right-wing government with capitalist ideals restored, increasing poverty and cynicism among today's youth, the question of whether it was all worth it is bound to arise. My interlocutors experienced nostalgia at various levels, for a woman that they had loved and admired and for a revolution that they had fought for. It was a double loss.

A grip on reality is the cornerstone of Nicaraguan action. Nora pursued an understanding of reality and a synthesis of it, throughout her life and work for the revolution. Yet most of the time I felt that the reality of Nora herself eluded me. This may not have surprised her since she saw her own life as an eternal conspiracy on behalf of the Nicaraguan people. Her life consisted of playing a series of different rôles on different stages - dutiful daughter, a good Catholic girl, a socialite, a Mata Hari, an advocate, a diplomat, a Madonna, a saint. Three of the most important dates in Nora Astorga's life seem to be more than coincidentally linked with images of women - the celebration of the Virgin Mary, the day of lovers, and international women's day. As a lawyer and as a revolutionary she always acted for the benefit of others and to a large extent her work was directed by others, by men. Did she in fact become a legend? Was she made into a star? Or was she a real woman that you and I can identify with?

The main aim of this book is to tell the story of an extraordinary woman living in extraordinary times, before the memory and sources fade. I have tried to put her firmly into context so that her life can illuminate the revolution and be illuminated by it. This is a book about Nicaragua, its achievements and its contradictions. I have tried to convey the inspiration that can be drawn from the Nicaraguan people and their story and the challenge this raises to our courage and commitment. Can any country be autonomous when the United States controls international politics? How far does this affect individual autonomy?

Writing the book raised all kinds of other questions for me - about women and revolution, about women in the public eye. In a world where revolutions are controlled by men can we talk about autonomy for women? In a world where the media objectify famous women, how can those women hold on to their authenticity as subjects? How dependent was Nora's success on the support of other women? These questions are relevant to women across the world.

Patricia Daniel
March 1997

Prologue

I knew that going back to Nicaragua would help me to see things more clearly. One aspect that was reinforced for me, as an atheist, was the influence of Catholicism in Latin America and in particular the importance of Mary, the mother of Christ, within the Catholic religion. Latin American women draw their strength from images of the Madonna but at the same time are constrained by them.

The trip that I took with my daughter happened to coincide with *Purisima*, the annual celebration of the Virgin Mary. It wasn't until then that I realised that this annual celebration directly precedes Nora Astorga's birthdate. This coincidence helped to highlight the connections between religion and Nora's life. Not only was Nora very much influenced by Catholicism as a child, but the cult of Mary also affected images of Nora as a woman and a public figure. In some photographs Nora (the Ambassador of Love, Life and Peace) was depicted with the same far away gaze as the Madonna. She was characterised with the same attributes - serenity, resolve and gentleness.

Purisima, the Feast of the Immaculate Conception, is the most important religious festival in Nicaragua. During the nine day period at the beginning of December, the people celebrate the Blessed Virgin Mary. Each household and each workplace has an altar with a statue of the Virgin, decorated with candles, fairy lights and sheaves of white irises. Any evening during *la novena* you will hear on the warm breeze chanting and singing, as families invite in their neighbours to celebrate with them. But it is on the ninth day, on the seventh of December, the Day of Happiness when the shouting (*la Griteria*) takes place:

What causes so much joy?
The conception of Maria!
I can't hear you! What causes so much joy?
The conception of Maria!

Unlike other religious ceremonies this is a time for raucous behaviour. There is also the giving and receiving of gifts. Poor families may save all year to be able to provide simple presents for their guests - a stick of sugar cane, an orange or a bag of sweets. Wealthy families measure the height of their devotion by the number of gifts they hand out.

The celebration highlights the importance of Mary in Catholic society and reflects the prevailing, conflicting views about women - the virgin mother, the bringer of redemption for the sins of Eve the temptress.

We all chant together:
> *Virgin and Mother of the World*
> *You were conceived without original sin*

Let us pray, says the Mother Superior:
> *Mary, the most beautiful, the most charming and gentlest of all God's creatures. In you there is no hypocrisy, no hate, no envy, no calumny, no injustice of any kind because God wanted his mother to be perfect so that all her (his) children, imitating her way of living would become like her. (1)*

The reading is taken from Genesis - the story of Eve, the serpent and the apple:
> *And unto woman God said: I shall greatly multiply your suffering in conception, with pain you shall bring forth your children.; your desire shall be to your husband and he shall rule over you ...*

The statue of Mary stands serenely on her altar, looking towards the light, her white robes flowing and her gold crown glowing. The second reading is taken from Luke, chapter 1, the immaculate conception of Jesus Christ:
> *You see the Virgin Mary heard the Word of God and submitted to the Lord's plans, although they were different from the plans she had. The*

Virgin always said 'Yes' to the Lord and dedicated her life to love and serve Him. Saint Isabel, full of the Holy Spirit, greets the Virgin Mary with these words: 'Blessed shall you be among women and blessed be the fruit of your womb.'

We all rise as one to our feet and pray:

> *Oh sublime Mother of God and of men, who gave life to God in your belly, nourishing him with your own blood, until he became life of your life... let me remember the joy of living, the enthusiasm for loving Christ and the sincerity to unite with my brothers and thus united, let us form a society where alone reign love and understanding, which only your son Jesus Christ can give.*

Ejaculation:

> *Jesus, Joseph and Mary, I give you my heart and my soul.*

And then we sing:

> *Conceived without flaw/ Full of grace/ Green olive/ White dove*
> *Iris that announces/ Peace to the soul*
> *Pure as the fragrant breeze of May*
> *Like the sweet smile of Eve*
> *as she strolled through the garden of Eden*

And the final eulogy:

> *Joseph is my guide and Mary is my advocate*
> *What causes so much joy?*
> *The conception of Maria!*

A Good Catholic Girl

Can dates really be significant in a person's destiny?

Nora Astorga seems to have been born at a propitious time. Her birthday was the ninth of December, the day after *Purisima* - the nine day celebration of the immaculate conception of the Virgin Mary. So the run-up to Nora's birthday was a national festival of joy, light and charity. And through all this ran the themes for the perfect Nicaraguan woman: purity, motherhood and advocacy, and the countervalues: pain, inequality, submission and injustice.

Apparently right from the beginning, Nora had a distinctive quality. She was born in the Baptist Hospital in Managua in 1948 and was a perfect baby who never cried and was never a nuisance. One of her aunts called her a little angel with a natural sweetness of character. She spent a happy childhood and was an intelligent and lively child who liked to enjoy herself, yet her mother, Doña Muriel, says that her face always had a sad expression with sleepy eyes. She seemed to look away into the distance, gentle yet detached, like the image of the Madonna. She didn't like to be cuddled or have her hair ruffled, but she wasn't a cold person, she was lively and enthusiastic. She loved by the head rather than the heart is what her mother said. Hers was an intellectual passion.

Nora was the first born. She was her father's favourite - his chance to pursue unrealised ambitions. Speaking about her parents Nora said, 'My father had an important influence on my life. From the time I was a child he kept telling me I was an individual who could study and become whatever I liked. He convinced me that being a woman was simply a descriptive characteristic not a limitation.' (1)

It is likely that Nora was particularly precious to her mother too, because she had lost a daughter the year before Nora was born. In contrast to her view of her father, Nora described her mother as a housewife who had only learned to cook and sew. But Doña Muriel doubtless helped with the administration of the family businesses, which included lumber exporting and a cattle ranch, as well as running the Astorga household, overseeing several family houses and their servants and looking after four children.

Her mother's skills were to prove invaluable to Nora throughout her life. She was always there to provide support for all of Nora's endeavours and without this support Nora's achievements would probably not have been possible. Although Nora doesn't talk much about her mother, they were very close. From Doña Muriel's point of view they were friends, a relationship that she was proud to have with all of her children.

One of Nora's contemporaries, Rosario Murillo, remembers that Doña Muriel was a smartly dressed woman who was very concerned about her appearance, and held afternoon teas for charity like a typical society lady.(2) Another of Nora's childhood friends, María Cristina Najlis, remembers that the whole family were very close. They would always gather together for special occasions like Christmas at their spacious airy house, thirteen kilometres up the main north road outside the steamy city of Managua, and Nora was a natural favourite with everyone.

On Nora's birthday there would always be a party. Nora's three younger siblings would be awkward in their brand-new clothes, and her handsome father would stand by to greet guests from the wealthy families of Managua and Nora's friends from school. There would be good food, beautifully presented and the whole affair was organised with precision and taste by Doña Muriel in an atmosphere of informality and slightly ironic good humour.

Nora attended a prestigious convent school - the Colegio Teresiano - run by nuns of the Carmelite order of St Teresa of Avila. The school, with its cool white and blue single storey buildings in the leafy shade is situated 5 kilometres up the Masaya Highway, high above the city, commanding the loveliest view of Managua. Lake Xolotlán below and Mount Monotombo rising from the water on the other side, both shimmer pale blue in the white heat of the day. The school is a tranquil place and the sunlight filters through the stained glass, casting liquid colours across the floors. The sharp smell of incense rises up to the arched ceiling of the simple white shell of the chapel and the rich notes of the organ resound, soaring with the sweet high voices of the girls' choir as they sing to Saint Teresa. 'Of course, religion marks you,' says her friend Guadelupe, who studied at the convent school in Granada. 'But is it scientific or mystical?'

In contrast to the other religious school for daughters of the wealthy, La Asunción, the Colegio Teresiano placed more emphasis on academic excellence than on 'finishing skills.' (3) Nora studied through the medium of English for most of her time there, to the delight of her father who was 'very gringista' (that is, pro-US).

Nora had high aspirations. She was always a perfectionist in her work and she studied hard. She turned in her homework on time and graduated as an honours student. She was remembered by her teachers as a pleasant, well-behaved, almost timid young girl. But María Cristina remembers that Nora was very popular at school among the pupils because she was so lively, in fact 'she never shut up!' (4)

Saint Teresa was a particular rôle model for Nora. She was a woman with a great capacity for communication who led an active social life and fought to reform the Carmelite Order, which during the 15th century had become a comfortable refuge for wealthy women. Teresa formed the order of 'barefoot Carmelites', who left behind their worldly goods and devoted their lives fully to God. Her struggle for what she believed in meant that she had to face the Inquisition.

It seems likely that the convent school had something to do with nurturing, not that expression of gentleness, sweetness and serenity which Nora had by nature, but the energy, firmness of resolve and transforming passion that lay behind it. (5)

The school year finished in February with 'promotion' ceremonies to congratulate students who progressed into the next grade and to award prizes. Then Nora would go east to the region of Chontales, to the family cattle ranch in Villa Somoza where she would visit her paternal grandparents. She had this in common with many other middle class girls, who were partly raised by grandmothers and great-aunts.

The famous revolutionary and poet Daisy Zamora, who was a student at the Colegio Teresiano one or two years behind Nora, writes on this very theme: 'The childhood we shared of hardworking grandmothers and ceremonious grandfathers in white linen suits and wide straw hats, who tolerated us with benevolence and gentleness.' (6) Nora was particularly close to her own grandmother with whom she had lived for some time as a child. In some ways they were very similar, physically undemonstrative, reflective and independent. According to her mother, when Nora was feeling tense about something, she would naturally go to her grandmother, to sit and talk things through with her. In the time they spent together, Nora learned a set of principles from her grandmother that she carried with her all her life. 'Do not measure people by what they have, but by how good they are,' *abuelita* used to say. 'You must always try to see what is inside a person and not just pay attention to appearances.' (*Caros vemos, corazones no sabemos* is a Nicaraguan proverb: we can see faces but we don't know hearts.)

Nora loved the Nicaraguan countryside. She could run freer there than in the city, with friends that she grew up with on the ranch. They would carry their bundled clothes, barefoot down the red dust track to the river, skipping past the young women who carried a baby on one hip, balanced a basket on their head and trailed a toddler behind them. The children could go splashing and swimming in deep pools after the washing was done and spread out on bushes to dry. And later, they would sit in the shade, calling out to the monkeys above, before collecting up the warm fresh clothes and clambering back in the late afternoon sun, with the little children of the village tagging along behind.

Many of the friends that Nora made then lived in two-room shacks with a small kitchen on one side. Outside in the neat little garden, as you sat on a wooden bench, a naked baby would toddle over to clamber into

11

your lap. Inside mothers bent over open fires, stirring rice and grilling *tortilla*. It was hot and dark in the tiny houses, with the only light provided by the sun shining through a small square hole in the wall. Chickens ran in and out, cheeping shrilly. In the room that she shared with her sisters and her little nephews, just large enough for the double bed, a friend would keep special treasures, hidden in a join in the wall or in a plastic bag hung up on a nail - a new school photograph or maybe a postcard from abroad.

Back at the *finca* Nora could sit on the veranda watching the trees grow dark on the mountain. Her grandmother, in her fresh flowered silk dress, peaceful now at the end of the day, would rock gently while Nora sat by her side on a little wooden stool clasping her knees under her chin and asking questions. The soft breeze rustled among the *malinche* blossoms as night finally fell and the full, silvery moon rose. At such times the future rises, vast, sweet, fertile and mysterious.

The social contrasts Nora perceived during the day time were already working uncomfortably inside her.

Her school days also played an important rôle in Nora's political awakening. She identified her debt to the nuns as follows: 'It was they who opened my eyes for the first time to a reality I didn't know.' This reality was poverty. Since she was a little girl she had gone to the marginalised neighbourhoods of Managua, on Thursdays and Saturdays, to give the catechism and to do charitable works - an apostolate.

The sun was bright over Monotombo. But now she went down the highway in the school bus, down into the city, through the centre and right to the edge of the lake itself. Acahualinca: it might mean 'the sewer' or 'the quagmire of weeds.' (I preferred the other interpretation of the name, 'place of the sunflowers', but saw none). (7)

The dirt streets are wide, the houses poor, made with rusted corrugated iron, paper, cardboard, strips of cloth, packing cases, sugar sacks, anything that can be used, for this is one of the poorest neighbourhoods in Managua where people learn to survive in poverty. The

12

city's sewerage empties out into the lake here, warned Sister. And there is effluence from the factories on the other side. The water is heavily polluted. Maybe that accounted for the shimmering, after all.

'Built on the banks of a shitty lake, Managua, you were never beautiful, sad city like an old whore whose ugliness maybe blossomed for a short while when you were young,' was how Daisy Zamora remembered it. (8)

Students from the Colegio Teresiano and boys from the Jesuit College, the Colegio Centroamericano, would spend evenings or part of their weekend giving health talks, teaching literacy classes or helping to build latrines or a small clinic in these neighbourhoods. It was acceptable to do this kind of 'social work' or 'good deeds' through the religious schools. Each group of children was accompanied by a nun or a priest. It was well motivated activity but paternalistic and did not receive a great response from the people. (9)

'Nora was my right arm, when we were doing the apostolate,' recalls one of her former teachers. 'She loved coming on Saturdays with the rest of the group.' Nora could dream of being a real doctor, as she helped hand out free medicine. But it was hard for a young girl to talk about hygiene when she saw the people living with open sewers. They had no clean drinking water, no running water at all and the women had to walk to the well, at least a mile, and back again. If they washed at the well, they had to wait and queue. The children had nothing. They slept on the earth floor, dressed in rags, and used the street as a toilet. No wonder they got ill.

As Nora spoke about hygiene, the women sat passively before her on borrowed chairs spread out in half-empty uneven rows. They fanned themselves as they listened, with babies at the breast beneath thin shawls or crawling in the dust at their feet. Inside their tiny sitting rooms, you could see signs of devotion. Gaudy pictures of the crucifixion, Madonna and Child, the Last Supper crowded in among mementoes from past festivals and funerals - a paper flower, a miniature wreath, old brown family photos.

A baby would keep up a constant dry wailing while its mother rocked and bounced it, rocked and bounced and lamented, 'You think we don't care about our children? You think we wouldn't do whatever is necessary to give them a better life? But what can we do? You see how we live here. Is God going to help us? What can you do? What I need is help for the baby, you see how she cries and cries, she's losing weight... I can't afford to take her to the doctor.' Diarrhoea was one of the most frequent causes of infant mortality. It attacks suddenly and within a few short days the child, dehydrated, can be dead.

The convent group used to take the children from the slums back to school to bath them. Nora carried out these tasks with enthusiasm and enjoyment: 'It didn't cost Nora anything to give the children love,' recalls her former teacher. 'The sacrifice, giving up her Saturday (they worked from 8am till 2pm), meant nothing to her. That was the way she was, always ready to help others.'

Experiences like this in the poor neighbourhoods affected Nora deeply and this was where she first learnt to identify with the Nicaraguan people. The Sisters managed to maintain their serenity, they did not seem to doubt their faith as they mingled in these lives dispensing charity, but Nora perceived that something more than charity was needed to change people's basic living conditions. She wanted her actions to achieve more than this. In her words, 'you're not giving much if what you give doesn't change society.'

However, it took Nora a long time to act on this perception. She enjoyed the catechism, but she also enjoyed an active social life in her teens. After the apostolate on Saturdays she would go to the private country club to swim, play golf and dance. Nora grew into a woman of great physical attraction. She was tall and slim with long dark hair, a pale heart-shaped face, and those dreamy eyes. With her looks, striking personality, sharp intelligence, self-possession and zany sense of humour, she was always popular.

'She had a lot of friends, both girls and boys, and when she made a friend, she was a friend for life,' says her mother. The name she was most often known by, 'la Norita' (little Nora) reflects the affection in which she was held but is also a joke, as she finally grew to a height of 5 feet 8 inches. A lot of boys were in love with her, but, in a sense, as her good friend Guadelupe put it, 'everyone always was.'

María Cristina Najlis was Nora's best friend right from the beginning of primary school until they graduated at eighteen with the *bachillerato*. She remembers that during her teens Nora fell in love with a different boy every week and was always devastated when it didn't work out... 'She was never able to find someone who really suited her, she was so suave, she had such a special personality. But it never took her long to get over it, because the next boyfriend was always the last, the only true love of her life!' Nora collected boyfriends like beads on a string and her mother would complain it was impossible to open the door of her house without falling over all Nora's admirers. (10)

'In lots of ways we led an empty life,' recalls María Cristina, 'concerned with clothes, parties and so on.' Yet Nora also had her serious side. She would spend a lot of time reading and liked to discuss what she read; she would also talk about her concerns for the country, about her future, what she wanted to become.

Although it was considered a 'sacrifice' for the young people to give up weekends to do social work, it was also a means of meeting members of the opposite sex, of forming relationships and exploring ideas together. The boys from the Colegio Centroamericano, like Joaquín Cuadra and Luis Carrión, had long conversations with the progressive priests who had connections with the liberation theology movement that was developing in Latin America. This movement promotes a preferential option for the poor, a liberating and empowering means of achieving justice and equality on earth rather than waiting for your reward in heaven. So, while they worked together in the *barrios* with Nora and her friends, they would discuss social

15

injustice and the need for political change in the country. As they grew older, the boys became more overtly political. They got hold of poorly mimeographed copies of *La Trinchera*, the clandestine newspaper of the Sandinista National Liberation Front (FSLN), the revolutionary organisation that had been set up in 1961, when Nora was going on thirteen, by Carlos Fonseca, Tomás Borge and Silvio Mayorga.

The aim of the FSLN was to abolish 'the entire system of exploitation and misery that oppresses our people.' (11) *La Trinchera* was published by Jorgé Navarro as part of the urban underground activities of the movement, while Carlos Fonseca established a base in the northern highlands, working with the *campesinos* and preparing guerrilla action. A small printshop turned out pamphlets like Carlos' *Social Classes in Nicaragua* along with primers for peasants, for whom the guerrilla created schools. One of the objectives of the FSLN was to 'eliminate once and for all the illiteracy that has immersed our people in the most degrading ignorance.' (12) Other actions included bank raids, which the FSLN, with their characteristic cheekiness, referred to as 'economic recovery'; they also took over *Radio Mundial* in Managua to denounce JF Kennedy's meeting with Central American presidents.

Jorgé Navarro was killed in the first major guerrilla combat in the Río Coco area in 1963 and the following year Carlos Fonseca was captured in Managua, tried and later deported to Guatemala. Already Carlos had attained legendary status. Reporters at his trial said that he employed different disguises, with or without glasses, wearing a hat or a cap. He was said to have disguised himself a poet, a monkey and a *centzontle* (Nicaraguan songbird)...

By the time Nora was about to begin her last year at school, the FSLN was becoming a public presence in Nicaragua. Nora describes herself as being politically completely naïve at this stage, she had no foundation in Marxism. She was also from a wealthy bourgeois background and a good Catholic girl, so it took her a long time to come to terms with the concept of armed rebellion. She may still have been looking at the future in terms of a good marriage.

One factor which goaded her into political activity was the negative position of her family. While Nora learnt confidence and ambition from her father, she also learnt in a negative sense - she was in continuous conflict with his ideas. Thus, from an early age Nora struggled to reconcile the contradictory values she experienced.

Nora's family on her father's side were Liberals, in other words they were capitalists and landowners. They supported the Somoza dynasty. Nora's paternal grandfather was a Liberal general and former Defence Minister and her father was also a military man and member of the National Guard. This army was developed specifically to protect the dictatorship and to deal with anyone who challenged it. Nora, as a child, was bounced up and down on the dictator's knee and given 20 cordobas. She may not have known exactly what the National Guard was responsible for, but she would see her father get up from the dinner table, dressed in his Guard uniform, fasten on his holster and leave the house without saying where he was going. This made a deep impression and guns terrified her.

When she came home from her apostolate as a child and began to ask ingenuous questions: 'Why are people poor, mummy? Why can't everyone have a nice little house with running water and a toilet?' she was told: 'Everything is as it should be, there is no need for change. There's a natural order in society. God's will be done. If it upsets you, you'd better stop and concentrate on your school work.'

As she continued with her social work, spending more time at it, becoming more involved, her father began to accuse her: 'What are you? A Communist?' 'But what's that?' she would ask, 'I don't even know what you're talking about.' Nora was just trying to be a good Catholic girl, 'who took Holy Communion every day, who went to mass every Friday and was a daughter of the Virgin Mary.' But his opposite view of the world, made so forcibly, in fact helped her to clarify her own ideas and to strengthen her

17

resolve. 'All I knew was that the country was poor, women were getting raped and there was nothing to eat. So I figured Somoza was no good...'(13)

Politics were discussed at home. There must have been talk about the Sandinistas because Nora remembered that the information she received about Sandino was the gringo image of a bandit wiping out co-operatives in the North (as opposed to the true version: a popular leader who defeated the United States marines in Nicaragua and was assassinated by Anastasio Somoza in 1934).

This radical ideological division within families is a feature which still characterises Nicaraguan life, at all levels of society. It has meant young people (in particular) working against their parents and siblings fighting against each other - both in armed combat and in the political arena. Yet family ties, especially to the mother, are still very strong and so it is usual to find family members providing practical support for each other and even living together despite their opposing political views.

From childhood, Nora, became 'an eternal accomplice of the people,' as Sofía Montenegro put it in her obituary. Nora saw this as her mission and to this end, she became, as she later used to tell her best friend, Guadelupe Salinas, 'an eternal conspirator against the contradictions and the counter-values of her society.' What also motivated Nora was the need she felt to reconcile the reality she herself lived with that lived by the people in the countryside and the people in Acahualinca. How could she form one sole reality in which everyone lived together? She said, 'The apostolate was not enough. There was a feeling of emptiness, I couldn't see any meaning in life, at least not in the circles I moved in - that's how I moved nearer to the FSLN position, without realising it...'

Paradoxically, Nora's privileged background was to provide invaluable training for her future work as a revolutionary, as well as equipping her with a social graciousness that was characteristic of her in all circumstances. Her status as most favoured child meant that it was a particular shock to the family when she made the radical change.

Rebellion

Nora started her last year at school in the year that student opposition to the régime became established. National Student Day was celebrated for the first time by a demonstration at the Universidad Centroamericana (UCA) , the Jesuit university in Managua. It was an eventful day. The early buses arrived from León, packed with students and workers, some sitting on the roof, some hanging off the ladders at the back, the heat rising inside as the sun rose. The crowd gathered at the university, chatting and trying to find some shade while they waited, and trying to find something to eat or drink. The food vendors at the gate had never enjoyed such trade. A crowd of young people sang, chanted and laughed as they paraded up and down with placards.

There were speeches, even though you couldn't hear much of them, and shouts and applause went up with the placards after almost every statement. It was exhilarating, though a little alarming because of the loss of personality in the unity. What was most alarming was the sight of the National Guard lined up on either side of the gates, silently watching, machine guns in evidence. (1) Casimiro Sotelo, a student at the UCA, had been visiting mining communities with Julio Buitrago, one of the founders of the FSLN. Both spoke out against the cruel exploitation of the workers by the foreign companies who owned the mines.

Casimiro was expelled from the university and more demonstrations followed. The Guard began using tear gas to suppress the students. On a peaceful march suddenly the Guard's jeeps would appear with the huge lights turned on you, and the thick smoke would burn in your eyes . Students were pursued by the Guard into churches and threatened there. Those identified were expelled temporarily from school. (2) Nora's own father was directly associated with this repression.

The appeal of the FSLN grew among young people. Their militants, imprisoned in Managua, were seen as heroes. Their daring raids on banks and supermarkets were bound to capture the imagination and impress.

Their manifesto *Sandino yes! Somoza no! Revolution yes, electoral farce no* ! was published in the run-up to the 1967 general election. It explained how the elections were rigged so that there was no chance for anyone but Tachito Somoza to win. The manifesto was signed by Carlos Fonseca, Oscar Turcios and Conchita Alday, the alias of Doris Tijerino, the leading woman revolutionary of those early days. (3)

At this stage, Nora still believed in peaceful resistance and she certainly was not ready to take part in illegal action. Instead she looked toward the Conservative Party as a legitimate possibility for change. 'The Greens', as they were known, represented the traditional Nicaraguan aristocrats and were more liberal than the Liberal Party. The Conservative leader, Fernando Agüero, had become an extremely popular presidential candidate. He was backed by a bourgeois coalition party, the National Opposition Union (UNO), a coalition brought about by the desire of many Nicaraguans to break the political and economic stranglehold of the Somoza dynasty. Nora got involved in Agüero's electoral campaign, which, of course, caused great problems at home in her Liberal family. Nora was still open with her parents about her political activity. Was this openness still ingenuous? Or was it now a deliberate rebellion? She remembered, 'There I was, saying I was a Conservative! I was breaking with family tradition!'

Despite the fact that her father was very strict, very *somocista*, it seems that throughout her teenage years Nora was not afraid to confront him. Alongside what might be seen as a naïve enthusiasm for social welfare, she showed herself to be strong and independent both intellectually and emotionally. Again, it was the conflicts she had at home over her involvement with the campaign that helped her to understand what it was that she herself wanted - a real social and political transformation.

The elections were due in February 1967. Agüero organised an opposition rally for 22nd January. He wanted to call for a general strike to support his demand that the elections be postponed until they could be carried out under a guarantee of impartiality. (4) There was a great turn-out. The streets were packed with 60,000 demonstrators - men and women, young and old, peasants, workers, professionals, people from out of town a little crumpled from sleeping overnight on the bus. The atmosphere was euphoric, there was singing, some spontaneous dancing, rather bawdy jokes. There was a feeling of oneness among the people, that spiritual uplifting of a shared belief, that going out of and beyond oneself, those feelings you might have on Friday morning at mass.

The midday sun beat down on the crowd and more and more people joined the throng, calling to acquaintances, pushing their way in, trying to get to the front, to be close to the hero of the day when he appeared. Vendors lined the pavements, taking advantage of the need to eat and drink. *El fresco! Tortillas! Chicharrón! Nacatamales! Mangos! Platanos!* came their hoarse cries. Music played out of loudspeakers, competing with the horns of cars trying to progress through the capital while the demonstration took over. *Con Fernando ando y con Agüero muero* (I walk with Fernando and I die with Agüero). The chant was taken up along the whole length of the avenue.

Then chaos broke out. The meeting had exceeded the permitted time-limit and the National Guard tried to disperse the Union's supporters as they paraded along the Avenida Roosevelt. Snipers on rooftops then fired on the soldiers and a bomb exploded in the National Telegraph Office. The crowd broke windows in the National Palace and widespread fighting developed in the streets of the capital, raging throughout the night. (5) The National Guard brought up tanks and gunned down the demonstrators. An estimated 500 people, of all ages, were killed in the massacre. Hundreds were kept in prison and tortured. Jacques Jacquier, the permanent representative of the International Red Cross in Latin America, found that a great number of these were not officially listed anywhere. However, there was a general amnesty for all political prisoners declared on the first of March.

The whole incident affected Nora deeply. 'I was really close. So many people I knew, so many dead, so many friends beaten, taken prisoner.' Terrifying as the violence was, it was not the only aspect of this event which made Nora question the way forward. What was worse was that the people were betrayed by Agüero. It was not so much that he had barricaded himself into the Gran Hotel while the shooting was going on outside - he and Pedro Chamorro, co-ordinator of the Union, were with hundreds of armed followers and they held over a hundred foreign visitors hostage until a truce was arranged and they were all allowed to go home. But later, after Somoza 'won' the elections, Agüero signed a pact with the dictator which Chamorro baptised in his paper (*La Prensa*) as *kupia kumi* - two hearts beating as one.(6) For many people, the massacre destroyed the credibility of the 'electoral farce' as a means of overthrowing the dictatorship. Nora says: 'I felt Agüero's betrayal in my flesh and told myself, this solves nothing.'

But Nora was not able to act on this realisation immediately. Her father, as a member of the National Guard, knew the risks she ran if she became identified as a rebel. He called her mad, he called her completely irresponsible, but he was terrified for her safety. Perhaps the massacre had also made him think about his own involvement. He decided anyway to send Nora out of the country, to the United States, because, as Nora said later, he hoped that there she would learn to become 'more reasonable.'

Nora's feelings against her father at this time must have been very strong. She had experienced at close hand what the Somocista Guards were capable of and her father was one of them. Then he made an autocratic decision about her future. Yet her mother indicates that Nora was not averse to the idea of studying abroad, although she might have preferred Europe to the United States, maybe Paris where Michèle Najlis (María Cristina's cousin) had gone after school a couple of years previously.

Nora graduated with honours in Science and Arts from the Colegio Teresiano in February 1967 and in March she was already on her way to

Washington. It was the first time she had been outside Nicaragua, away from her family, leaving the protection of the convent school and the beauty of the mountains behind. She describes herself as 'just a young provincial girl.' Yet her experiences of violence, poverty, corruption and hypocrisy had in some sense already exiled her from her given reality.

There was certainly an element of excitement and adventure. Nora had always had an avid curiosity for the world and its people and now she was going to a new country where she could make new friends and use her English. She may have felt she was escaping from the contradictions and conflicts which she had grown up with. It must have been exciting to be gone from all that for a while, running free. Indeed she did have a great deal of freedom. Although Nora had an aunt in Washington, María del Carmen, and was going to the Catholic University, it seems there was no attempt on the part of her father to keep tabs on her activities. 'She could look after herself,' says her mother. 'She lived in the university dorm where she made friends with whoever she pleased. She was so independent.'

It was not at all unusual in those days for young Nicaraguans of the middle and upper classes to go abroad to complete their education at a foreign university. The famous poet Gioconda Belli, for instance, was sent to the United States to study Advertising and Journalism. One reason was the lack of higher education in Nicaragua itself. However, in the sixties, the Jesuits established the Universidad Centroamericana (UCA) in Managua and the National University (UNAN) was enlarged and a second campus was set up in Managua. This meant more young women were gaining access to higher education within the country.(7)

Young people concerned with social reform began to debate the alternatives for university study. One view was that you'd spend four years abroad, get depoliticised, lose interest and come back a technocrat. Others said, no, that it was important to have the chance to study abroad and it shouldn't be wasted. It was an opportunity to offer more to Nicaragua.(8)

23

Nora followed a similar line of reasoning: 'I decided to study Medicine because I believed it was a profession where I could work for social change.' Given her knowledge of the conditions in which many Nicaraguan people lived - the risk to children's lives and the neglect of women's health in the poor neighbourhoods - the decision seems a logical one.

Her problem was that she was squeamish - too soft-hearted even to cut into a little animal in the dissecting class. 'I went through agony: how was I going to cut into a person?' When she went into hospital for observation, she felt faint. 'I couldn't cope with human pain.' There was no way that she could contemplate practising surgery. Her tutor finally took her aside one day and said: 'Look, I get the impression that you don't really have many of the qualities you need for this work. Find yourself another profession.' Nora was relieved.

This story is an interesting one. Maybe Nora recounted it with a certain amount of wry humour against herself. She certainly learnt something about suffering later. There is no question that in the years that followed she had to grit her teeth and come to terms with the pain and death of close friends and comrades. And although she did overcome the squeamishness, she never lost her soft heart and the capacity to cry.

This was also probably the first time that Nora, the perfectionist, had actually failed at anything related to her studies. She enrolled at the Catholic University of America in Washington in September 1967 to study Sociology but in fact spent less than a year on the course, leaving in May 1968.

While Nora's dream of becoming a doctor for the Nicaraguan people was unrealised, she did not get depoliticised. In fact, her time in the United States was very important in her political development. From time to time she would receive news from home about the FSLN and their collaborators. Even before she started her Sociology course, came the news of Pancasán. The FSLN had been working up there in the north for months, organising a guerrilla base with peasant support. On August 13th 1967, the National Guard engaged them in combat. It was a bad day for the FSLN: they lost thirteen of their leaders. However, with their usual style of optimism, they claimed this as a political victory, announcing that it had focused attention on them as the most credible opposition to the dictator.

Casimiri Sotelo, the student who had been expelled from the UCA, had gone underground. In November he was caught in a Managua neighbourhood *barrio*, Monseñor Lezcano, with three other militants. They were taken away to the dungeons under the Presidential Palace and assassinated there.

The following year, on 28th September 1968, one of the lecturers at the UCA, Ricardo Morales, was caught engaged in clandestine activity as a member of the urban guerrilla group working under Julio Buitrago. He was kept in the military prison in the centre of Managua, La Aviación. He had been involved with the FSLN for a couple of years, inspired by his *compañera*, Doris Tijerino, (alias Conchita), the militant from Matagalpa.

As well as news from home there was certainly plenty going on in the United States while Nora was there. The news was filled with the Vietnam War, although the news didn't always reflect reality: 'Another successful attack on Viet Cong forces in the North. General Westmoreland is predicting that, with the intensified counterinsurgency effort, the Communist menace will be subdued by Christmas and the occupied territories liberated.' Vietnam was a prime example of the United States fighting because it hated to lose, possibly an even greater motive than anti-communist fervour.

We don't know how much Nora unravelled about the Vietnam War and what comparisons she was able to make at this stage between the United States' involvement in Asia and the United States in Central America and Cuba; between the rural campaign of the Viet Cong and the operation of the FSLN guerrillas back home. She must certainly have been studying alongside young North Americans whose lives were overshadowed by the war - the losses, the rumours, the threat of the draft.

The late sixties was the period when student protest against the war intensified in the United States and everyone was affected by this, particularly in Washington which was the locus for major events.

Nora clearly remembered the civil rights movement and more than anything, the racism of the United States. Not long after she arrived in Washington, Martin Luther King began to speak out against Vietnam. There was a series of peace marches, demonstrations and acts of civil disobedience. Race questions were raised in the Senate. In the summer of 1967 race riots broke out. The Klu Klux Klan were active and so were Black Power. Segregation in education was instituted in Alabama partly as a result of the riots. And a press campaign to discredit King was launched.

The Abraham Lincoln Memorial in Washington celebrates the notions of equality, freedom and justice. It was the site of demonstrations for equal rights during the sixties and it was here that Martin Luther King gave his famous 'I have a dream' speech in 1963. Protesters would sprawl on the grass by the huge 'reflecting pool' at the base of the memorial steps, enjoying the sunshine until speeches began.

In Washington a third of the population were African American and they mixed freely with whites in public places but there were still few African American students at university. Most of these would go to Howard, the university down the road from CUA. In many states, segregation was still the norm. These social contrasts as well as the hostility between white and black that made a deep impression on Nora: '... this racism that I'd never known in Nicaragua. Things like this deepened my uneasiness. And a political understanding was born in me. An awareness that not only in my own country things were wrong, but everywhere.'

Nora herself was subject to racism; to many North Americans she was just a 'spic', one of a number of Hispanic students at CUA, especially from Puerto Rico. And as people were lumped together, so were their

26

countries; she remembered one of her Sociology professors writing off Nicaragua as another 'banana republic.' (9)

The year following Nora's arrival in the United States, King was assassinated when he went down to Memphis to support a garbage workers' strike. On April 4th 1968 he was killed by a sniper bullet while he stood on a motel balcony. Nora said, 'I was in Washington when they killed him. I can't forget the reaction of the black community.' A wave of racial violence spread across the States, much of it quelled by the National Guard. Beyond the grief and anger must have been the same feeling of powerlessness, that sense of betrayal and manipulation that Nora had felt a year or so earlier in Managua, after the January massacre. There had to be another way...

As Nora had struggled with 'reality' in Nicaragua, this was also a problem in the United States. The cover-up of what was really happening in Vietnam in the name of democracy and the media manipulation of Martin Luther King were only two examples of what she saw as the tremendous level of disinformation. As she put it later, 'The whole society seems to be geared towards concealing what's important or making sure that people don't get interested in realities outside their own little world. That's why I really admire those North Americans who fight for the civil rights of minorities, for disarmament... The conditions for those kind of struggles are not easy there.'

Nora herself later would become an object of the media, of the United States press in particular, subject to images of herself and her country that did not reflect her own reality.

She was in Washington during the election campaigns of 1968 and she read about the assassination of Robert Kennedy and Nixon's consistent success in the primaries and presidential nomination at the Republican Convention in August.

Nixon's election platform included action on Vietnam and, regarding Latin America, he wished to 'encourage progress of economic integration

27

in order to promote industrialisation and economic diversity' as a response to the present poverty. He wished to reconfirm the Monroe Doctrine (the core principle being that no hostile foreign power will be allowed bases or allies in the region) and to realign overseas aid with foreign policy: in other words only offer aid to countries who were friendly to the United States. (10)

Interestingly, Nora was to look back on her time in Washington as some of the best years of her life and to remember Washington as the most beautiful city in the world after Managua. For a provincial girl from Central America, Washington was a good choice. The first modern city to be built as a capital, it is a city of vistas, of gardens and rivers, of elegant buildings, simple monuments and gracious avenues, with no industry, no sky-scrapers and no slums.

Nora particularly loved the famous basilica at the Catholic University, the National Shrine of the Immaculate Conception, which is the largest Catholic church in the United States and is a sumptuous celebration of Mary with magnificent mosaic work in deep blues and gold. There is a reproduction of Titian's painting of the Assumption, a bronze sculpture of the holy family resting on their flight to Egypt and a mosaic of Our Lady of Guadelupe 'fair as the moon, bright as the sun' with farmers and children bringing gifts to her.(11) The academic year was opened by a mass in the basilica and the Immaculate Conception was celebrated on the 8th of December.

Nora loved to walk along the bank of the river Potomac where the Japanese cherry trees blossom in springtime, watching the squirrels dart over the grass, or visit the art galleries and museums. One of her favourite paintings was Renoir's Luncheon of the Boating Party, in the Phillips Collection - this is a scene of bourgeois relaxation, men and women mingling at their ease and the wine flowing freely. (12)

At CUA there was the trivia of activities organised around the fraternities and sororities - formal dances, cruises down the Potomac, the

28

fraternity 'queen' attended by a court of fraternity sweethearts, female students rehearsing to be cheerleaders for male sporting events - which Nora characterised as 'the most superficial time I've ever experienced'. (13) There was heavy snow over winter 1967, making the campus look like a Christmas card, the gymnasium was turned into a concert hall with lights and a tall tree and the orchestra and choir combined to provide a special Christmas performance.

Although it was a relatively conservative university, there was also political activity at CUA. In the summer of 1968 the students went on strike for 6 days to protest on behalf of a Reverend Charles Curran whose contract was not extended because he had expressed 'liberal views' on modern Catholicism.(14) Throughout that year the student newspaper, *The Tower*, reported on race issues and curriculum developments within the university to include African American history, 'racial education' and peace studies.

While she was studying in Washington Nora came into contact with the international diplomatic circle at the Nicaraguan Embassy. At receptions she could meet up with other Nicaraguans resident in the United States, diplomats and other students, from the middle class and the aristocracy of Nicaragua: 'Nicas always seek out Nicas,' explains her mother. This was an elegant part of life, but another arena where her growing political understanding conflicted with the attitudes of many of the people she had contact with.

What was Nora's own reality at this time? She learnt a lot by observing, waiting, and watching the rise and fall of other heroes. Perhaps she was deliberately careful about participating in political activities.

It wasn't until 1969 that her parents decided that Nora had forgotten all her 'crazy ideas' and that it was safe for her to return home. She was keen to do so: 'King's death reminded me I didn't belong there, but in Nicaragua.' (15)

She enrolled in the Catholic University in Managua (the UCA), as was expected, and this time she chose to study Law. Her morale at this time was high. She was home, she was twenty, she was self-sufficient (or believed herself so to be) and she was on top of the world. However, despite her political awakening in the United States, Nora still had a lot to learn about reality in her own country: 'I still had a naïve belief in the idea of justice in Nicaragua and, consequently, entered the Law School with a lot of illusions. I couldn't have known the atrocities which passed for justice in Nicaragua.' (16)

Forward with the Front

When she enrolled at the UCA, Nora entered into a period of her life which was characterised by intense activity and radical changes.

The UCA is situated at the foot of the Masaya Highway. It is a modest looking institution with a simple white two-storey administration block and rows of classrooms. The campus is pleasant and shady with broad walkways and flowering bushes. There used to be a students' cafeteria with small round metal tables on a covered terrace. Outside the front gate was the busy bus stop and across the road a small bar called Kings which had a striped awning and sold beer in large jugs. At the side entrance another kiosk sold *chicharrón* and yucca chips.

The UCA had been set up in the 1960s by the Somoza family and the right-wing as a counter-revolutionary manoeuvre - to put a brake on student politics by introducing a private Catholic bourgeois institution into the higher education sector. Ironically, students at the UCA helped a great deal to strengthen the revolutionary movement, fired as many were by ideas from liberation theology and a readiness to denounce injustice. Their worst excesses were supported by their fathers - because of parental love not political collusion - and a great social pressure from the middle classes in the face of the Somoza government actually helped students to achieve political goals.

Although at this stage the FSLN was not the only leftist group organising against the dictatorship, nor was it the largest, it began to gain ascendance through this penetration into the middle class. In the earlier stages of organisation, the working class students who attended the National University (the UNAN) mistrusted the religious ethos as well as the class origins of the student movement at the UCA but this proved to be an error.(1)

In the Law Faculty, Nora met up with her schoolfriend Marisol Morales, Gloria Gabuardi, who was also from Managua, and her childhood friend,

31

Guadelupe Salinas, who had studied at the convent school in Granada. Other students at the UCA at that time included Milú Vargas, also studying Law, and Daisy Zamora who studied Psychology. All these women shortly became involved in the revolutionary struggle.

Nora was very worried when she returned from the United States because she had already missed more than a year of the course, remembers María Cristina Najlis. However she applied herself to studying and managed to cover two years' work in one - a good indication of her intellectual competence and her capacity to achieve under pressure.

It is not surprising that it was from the Law Schools in Managua and León that many of the prominent revolutionaries were produced. Guadelupe Salinas said, 'The law is the highest level of domination in the social structure. Through changing the law, you can transform reality. On the other hand, those who wish to keep the status quo, to maintain socio-economic control of the country, are like Egyptian mummies... People involved in the law are either very revolutionary or very reactionary.'

Influential lecturers in the UCA included Ernesto Castillo Martinez, who was then Public Prosecutor, and Manolo Morales Peralta, who was Marisol's uncle. Through them, the students were introduced to Marx, Castro, Lenin. They worked as volunteers in the *bufete popular*, set up by Manolo, which provided free legal aid to the public. Guadelupe Salinas remembers that, 'It gave us the chance to open the door and look out at what was happening in the street.'

Manolo would also give them some topic to discuss, for instance a current court case, and Guadelupe explains that, 'we would take turns in class to provoke one of the other lecturers, the Head of the Supreme Court, one of the mummies, who claimed his teaching and his job were two separate and distinct activities... Nora, me, our friend Carlos Agüero, one of us would get kicked out of class and then another of us would take up the challenge'.

Guadelupe also recalls intense discussions outside class, articulating the future. They may have been studying law, but they were also interested in reading French anthropology and existentialist philosophy. For example, Sartre's position on being and not being: how was it possible for everyone to become at the same time the subject in a shared reality? This question had implications not only for the future of the country - for justice and equality in its political and economic relations - but also for personal relationships - the future for woman as subject in her own life as opposed to woman as object in a man's world and the possibility of a union between the sexes which was fair and equal. This intellectual exploration was linked with a desire for action. As Guadelupe recalls, 'we studied thousands of plans to get rid of the dictatorship: becoming a spy like Mata Hari; getting a job as a cook and poisoning Somoza's food.'

Nora had been away for two years, becoming more aware of what was wrong in the world, watching and waiting. 'Although I had not known the Sandinista National Liberation Front (FSLN) directly before, it was almost natural that I would begin to look to them as an option when I returned to Nicaragua.'

Nora had become close friends with Rosalina Estrada who was married to Alfonso García, the President of the Students Centre and a member of the FSLN. It was Alfonso who first began to goad Nora into becoming actively involved. Then her classmate Carlos Agüero, whose code name or *nombre de guerra* (warname) was Rodrigo, was given the job of encouraging her to join the FSLN. 'He came and talked to me. He made me question who I was, what I was doing and what I had the ability and obligation to do.'(2)

The FSLN approach to individuals they saw as potential collaborators followed a pattern of gradual approximation. They wanted to be sure of a person's commitment before involving them at a higher level. Some people needed more time than others. Nora's friend Milú, for example, was approached by Alejandro Gutiérrez almost immediately she started university and he asked her if she wanted to join. 'He didn't have to do a lot to convince me,' she remembers. (3) She was elected class representative in her first year and became involved in student action.

It seems Nora took a little longer to make her decision. 'They never tried to force me to do anything beyond my real capacity. They would give me things to read and let me form my own conclusions, guiding me along.' (6) There was a clandestine library that did the rounds of the campus. So Nora studied Sandinism and its values as well as law. She studied the reality of Nicaragua in her search for answers.

One of the first books Nora read was *El Pequeño Ejército Loco* by Gregorio Selser (5), a book that was an important introduction for many of the students. Selser's books describe and analyse in detail the story of Sandino and his 'crazy little army' between 1926 and 1933. They highlight on one hand the extent of United States intervention in Central American affairs and the depths of terror to which the United States will go in order to maintain control. On the other hand they demonstrate the possibilities of organised resistance - what can be achieved if people really believe in the importance of national sovereignty and freedom from oppression. It was at this time, Nora said, 'I started to really identify with Sandinism and to understand that this was where I could and should put my energies.' (6) Carlos Agüero spent a lot of time talking to her on these matters for a few months until he left to join the guerrilla forces in the mountains. By this time Nora had begun collaborating.

As a young wealthy woman, Nora had her own house and her own car and, as daughter of a middle class Liberal family, she had access to wherever she wanted to go. In other words, in common with other young women from the same social circles, she had 'good cover'. Her early contributions therefore included providing a place for meetings, transporting comrades and taking messages. Her war name at that time was María.

Even at this level of collaboration there was a complicated system of secret signals, notes folded in specified ways and many other minutiae of security measures which are described with some humour in Gioconda Belli's novel *La Mujer Habitada* (A Woman Possessed, published in 1988). Only a small number of comrades would operate together in the cell

34

system and were only allowed to use code names. As Daisy Zamora sadly commented, 'we would only recover our real names if we died in action.' (7)

The risks run by collaborators were not trivial. On July 15th 1969 Conchita (Doris Tijerino) had been captured and Julio Buitrago killed when the Guard found out his Managua safe house and sent in 400 troops to besiege it with machine guns, tear gas, and hand grenades, backed up by fighter aircraft and a Sherman tank. Julio resisted to the end, singing the Sandinista hymn as he died. The Guard surrounded the house for hours and kept giving the order to surrender through the loudspeaker. The house remained full of smoke. They kept getting no answer and so they kept bringing in more tanks: the Guards were quaking - but nobody was answering - because Julio had, of course, already died. (8)

Conchita was in the house, too, and managed to evacuate Gloria Campos and her daughter. When she returned, she was caught and held in a jeep, from where she watched the rest of the battle. They took her to the dungeons in the National Palace where she was imprisoned until the end of 1972, tortured and raped. The dictator had a private dungeon beneath a dining room where statesmen and their cronies sipped expensive wine; as an after dinner pastime, Somoza and his friends would come down and rape the women prisoners. (9)

It was clear that someone had been giving away secrets, because the Guard had found out about another safe house in Managua, way across town in Santo Domingo. They killed another three militants on the same day and in the same way. Julio Buitrago's death was televised on several successive nights, presumably in the belief that this would undermine the revolutionary movement. This plan backfired, although the loss of the leader of the urban guerrilla force was, of course, a blow for the FSLN. Omar Cabezas, who was at that time President of the famous Association of Law Students at the university in León, points out that seeing Julio's heroism over and over again 'made us want to cry - but at the same time we felt that we had an indestructible strength.' (10).

35

Nora's particular responsibility was to Oscar Turcios, another member of the FSLN Directorate. Oscar had been involved in Pancasán and before that had fought with the Guatemalan resistance as a squadron leader. At this time he was working between Managua and León. Nora would act as his driver, find safe houses and carry messages for him.

Nora worked with Oscar Turcios for four years and remembered him with great affection and respect as a person who helped her to develop politically and personally. 'Oscar was able to see, behind the façade of self-sufficiency and liberalism, I had other things inside me. And it was those things he helped me to develop.'

Nora employs her characteristic irony when describing an early image of herself, looking back with the hindsight of a political career to her own naïveté at this stage. 'When I got involved with the FSLN, I had a romantic idea, almost a movieland idea, of what it was. I wanted to be a sort of Tanya the guerrilla. I was a rebel without a cause. Now it makes me smile.' She claims she never had time to study Marxism. However, there were many definite aspects of life that she was rebelling against: her own life, her own circle, their values and privileges. Maybe she was still unable to articulate all this.

She said, 'Oscar taught me about the dedication I would need if I were to join the FSLN. But at the same time as he encouraged me to move closer to the organisation, he also seemed to understand our limitations. He was enormously patient.' (11) Although Nora was still only on the periphery of the organisation, she learned that all tasks had their significance. 'Oscar showed me how decisive an ant's work can be, although one never sees it. My work was like that and it allowed him to do a number of very important things for the struggle.'

However, at this stage, Nora's participation was what she described as 'timid', in comparison to that of other comrades.

Involvement in the revolutionary struggle was one way in which young women like Nora were able to find their own reality - something which had eluded them since childhood - through action and adventure. It gave their life a meaning, it gave them the sense of a new freedom, the chance to work for change, to create a new society, to develop, as Gioconda Belli put it in an interview, 'new relations of production which will allow a new man, a new woman to come into being.' (12). Once the opportunity had arisen to see themselves in this new light, the only way for women to be free had to be through revolution.

This rebellion, which enabled them to reveal themselves, to get rid of the façade, also enabled women to experience their sexuality as a natural part of life. 'I was singing out of my pleasure at being alive, of feeling glad to be a woman and living in a time when things were happening which promised such important changes,' Gioconda Belli went on to explain about her early poetry.

Paradoxically, however, those women involved in the organisation still led a double life, because they had to work undercover or to use their cover carefully to further the aims of the struggle, following the rules for safety, still conspirators against the counter-values of the world they inhabited. In many ways they weren't allowed to reveal themselves.

For Nora another problem was the conflict between her image of herself as a guerrilla fighter and the fact that she couldn't stand the sight of blood. She still adhered to the concept of peaceful, as opposed to armed, resistance.

She was also busy on another front, in student politics. She became secretary of the Student Centre at the UCA. She remembered the first time in her life she had to make a speech in public at the university, she 'trembled from head to toe.' Strangely enough for someone studying law - and for someone who was to go into the diplomatic arena - she felt that public speaking was never one of her strengths.

The Revolutionary Student Front (FER), the university arm of the FSLN, had continued to grow and become involved in different sectors. Towards the end of the 1960s it had taken over the Presidency of the

University Centre (CUUN) in León which meant that the FER/FSLN were directly involved in representing students before the University governing body. From that time on, the students had a structural link with the FSLN.

The climate of the university was primarily anti-Somocista. The students were all aware of student massacres, the multiple repression of students, the importance of the fight for university autonomy and the success of the bid for universities to get 2% of the national budget. (13) In the early 1970s the activity of all the student groups centred around the movement to obtain the freedom of political prisoners (who were Sandinistas). Ricardo Morales, who had already served out his sentences, was being kept in jail in Nicaragua. Carlos Fonseca was imprisoned in Costa Rica. An international campaign spearheaded by the French philosophers Jean-Paul Sartre and Simone de Beauvoir was launched in 1970, for the release of Carlos Fonseca. 'Those were years of intense student struggles,' Nora said of this time. (14) That was when the first take-overs of churches and hunger strikes took place.

The movement was nation-wide, involving mainly students although many working class organisations joined later. Some of the priests at the UCA, including Fernando Cardenal, took part in the occupations. The campaign, calling for an end to repression, attracted thousands of people. It was directed by the FSLN and inspired by slogans such as: 'The people united will never be defeated.' (15)

'The occupation of churches was the first major act of significance,' explains Guadelupe, 'and it had national repercussions. It was planned so that the take-over of cathedrals in cities around the country was simultaneous - Nora, me, William Huper in Managua, the FER in León and so on.'

When a large photograph appeared in *La Prensa* of Nora occupying the Cathedral, Nora's mother was horrified at this notoriety and blasphemy. What was her wayward daughter doing now? She even came down to the Cathedral where Nora was fasting and called her 'a disgrace' to the family. (16) Even Nora's best friend from school, María Cristina, was amazed at 'this great change' that had happened since Nora returned from the United States.

At the UCA the fight was linked to student demands for university reform, in particular the removal of the Rector, who was very right wing, and the University was also occupied.

The Guard reacted to the peaceful protests in their usual way. They broke up marches with tear gas and physical threats, they burst into churches with machine guns, they even came onto the UCA campus several times in their jeeps, brandishing their weapons, to intimidate the students. The students' parents were often well connected and tried to protect their children. (Guadelupe's uncle was a deputy in the government and her brother was mayor of Granada, for example). But there was always the risk of stray bullets and afterwards the repression got worse and young people began to disappear or end up in jail. (17)

Nora went back to her old school to seek support from the pupils and the nuns for the campaign. But she did not receive the answer she expected. 'This is not what we taught you,' the nuns said. 'This is the result of the education I received from you; don't complain, I have had no influence but yours!' she told them. But they didn't agree with the conclusion she had reached and appealed to her to be a 'good follower of St. Teresa'. Nora went away feeling that it was they who had not drawn the logical conclusion from their teachings (as other religious teachers such as Uriel Molina and Fernando Cardenal had done): hadn't she become a radical reformer like Teresa? Her attachment to the school and to the nuns, to religion itself, began to diminish.

Nora met Jorgé Jenkins Molieri after the first occupation of the Cathedral. Jorgé was a Biology student at the UNAN in León and had taken over as Student Representative from Jaime Wheelock. He was also a great friend of Alfonso García who had first introduced Nora to the FSLN.

Nora and Jorgé met at a political meeting held one night at the UCA to plan protest action. Fernando Cardenal and William Huper were there as well as Nora's friend Rosalina Estrada. Jorgé's picture of Nora is very revealing: 'Nora was really pretty, in a fantastic miniskirt and her shy demeanour. She didn't participate much in the discussion, unlike the rest of us. She was shy and melancholic, almost as if she was absent or perhaps too present, in order to show her attentiveness. She stood out from the rest precisely because she didn't stand out. No way do I mean to say that she appeared stupid, rather that her silence was respectful, it was the silence of someone who thought deeply about what she did. Someone who didn't take things lightly.'

After the meeting, Jorgé, who was there representing the FER, spoke to Nora and William Huper about joining the FSLN, not realising that they had already been approached. He did know that Nora's father, once a Lieutenant in the National Guard, had rebelled against Somoza since the January 1967 massacre. 'Nora captivated me immediately,' says Jorgé. They started to date, meeting at the University Club in Managua (the Student Centre) and in his grandfather's house on the highway to the south, where Nora also lived.

'A lot of our conversation was about social themes. The poor, the dispossessed, injustice, repression.. Our vision of society was fortunately romantic and our only alternative was the FSLN. And also our vision of the FSLN was romantic - again fortunately - since at that time no-one alive could seriously imagine a military victory against the National Guard and the whole Somocista government apparatus.'

As Jorgé was the UNAN student representative to the FSLN, he was 'supposedly at a higher level of political development than me,' recalled Nora. He was a pre-militant, that is, soon eligible for full membership of the organisation, while Nora was just a collaborator. With hindsight Jorgé is able to criticise his own political position at this time and that of his colleagues in the FER. 'I suppose we were really dogmatic. We thought we were masters of Marxism, as if this meant we were licensed to be called revolutionaries. In fact history shows that most Marxists were never revolutionaries and many Christians were. Anyway, in those days, we used to recite the Marxist liturgy on any conceivable occasion, perhaps without understanding much of Marxism itself. We would recite the philosophy manuals on dialectic materialism, bits of political economy and a few historical passages of the Bolshevik revolution. We didn't know how all this could be translated into concrete action for us to liberate the Nicaraguan people from poverty and oppression.'

Nora took part in the philosophy seminars and Jorgé talked to her a lot on the subject of Marxism when they were alone. But Nora approached things differently, even at that stage. 'Nora was a person who wanted to learn, but she didn't particularly want to learn by reading and studying. Her knowledge of Marxism was basic and this didn't seem to bother her much either. She learnt by intuition rather than by knowledge of the tools of socio-political analysis. She was a woman of social action, and in this she had enormous talent - as well as an exceptional gift with people which enabled her to get close to them,' Jorgé concluded.

Jorgé was handsome and charming and played the guitar. And Nora was an elegant confident young woman of great physical attraction. They fell madly in love. They must have met up when she travelled to León with Oscar Turcios, because Carlos Tünnermann recalls first meeting Nora at the university there.

Very shortly after this, Nora and Jorgé decided to get married. Maybe it was a deeply passionate attraction which was the deciding factor; they married after only knowing each other three months. Maybe it was the feeling that life was too precious to waste; Jorgé might soon go into the guerrilla and be killed. Maybe Nora believed she had found the new man and this was the chance she had been looking for - a new relationship between man and woman, between two people who shared a political commitment to social change. Maybe she imagined they would be a revolutionary partnership.

41

Possibly it was Jorgé who pushed for an early marriage. Nora recalls telling him that she didn't want anything to get in the way of her political life. 'Okay, we'll get married,' I told him, 'but my political life comes first.' (19) And maybe it was because Nora was already pregnant; their first daughter, Muriel, was born before she graduated. But, probably it was a combination of all these possibilities.

Given the speed of the affair, the announcement came as a complete shock to her parents, particularly to Nora's father who had a heart attack the next day (20). Segundo Astorga had retired from the National Guard so that he could concentrate on the ranching business, but he was still a Liberal. 'We didn't really know about Jorgé's political activities,' says Doña Muriel, 'but of course we suspected, we were anxious for Nora, we knew it was very dangerous. Yet in the end we accepted the marriage.'

This is one of the many examples where Nora made a decision which her family had to accept. Despite their opposition to the relationship, her parents attended the wedding - a traditional Catholic ceremony.

In some ways it seems that Nora's mother was also 'an eternal conspirator,' despite her own political opposition to Nora's activities. Doña Muriel colluded, not only in reconciling her husband to Nora's choice of partner, but also in concealing from him what she suspected about Nora's own involvement in the FSLN. She remembers, 'Those were hard times, my husband was a Somocista and I could imagine what my daughter was up to, I was walking a tightrope... We even had three boys hiding out in this house (the Managua residence) for three days.'

It wasn't only Nora's parents who disapproved of the marriage. Oscar Turcios himself thought it was ill-advised, but Nora refused to listen even to her mentor. In addition, she almost lost her oldest friend because of her relationship with Jorgé. María Cristina recalls that she herself had recently got married. 'Nora used to come to my house (also on the *Carretera Sur*) along with members the FSLN, to discuss their upcoming operations... but after she started going with Jorgé, since I didn't like him, we didn't talk much, well, he was the one who was always talking, the only time I could talk to Nora was when he wasn't there!'

Despite this, the early days of marriage were heady days. Guadelupe Salinas remembers the best friends and their partners would go out all together to have fun, 'three and three', Nora and Guadelupe with their new husbands and Gloria Gabuardi with Chichú Fernandez. Student friends and collaborators would come round to meet at their house, one by one after dark, in soft soled trainers, giving the secret signal quietly at the back door in the shadow of the bushes.

Alone, Nora and Jorgé would discuss politics - 'he helped me grow and mature' - and, since at this time they were both active politically, the creative force that drove their work for change was an integral part of their physical and emotional life together. They could make love and dream of a future where their children would walk free in a free country.

Separation

Because of the cult of holy motherhood in Nicaragua, pregnancy can be a very rewarding experience. The bigger you become, the more people (the taxi driver, the woman selling *tortillas*) will say you are beautiful. And it was the first time for Nora, a new experience, another aspect of her revolutionary creativity and another direction for her to grow in. She continued her studies throughout her pregnancy, something that shocked her friend María Cristina: 'she just went around the university with her great belly, what a scandal!'

Nora also continued to work for Oscar, in fact the pregnancy improved her cover. However, later in her pregnancy he became concerned for her safety and her work for him ceased. Jorgé also continued with his work for the FSLN. He would sometimes have meetings or operations (he would not have been allowed to tell her details) and not return till morning. Or he might rise before dawn and Nora would wake to find him gone, with the shape of him still visible in the sheets.

On 30th October 1971, Nora gave birth to a baby girl, in the small private Baptist hospital near the National Palace. She was named Muriel for Nora's mother and was the culmination of the busy joyfulness of those few months.

Even after the birth of her daughter Nora continued to be involved in the student campaign for autonomy and at around this time it began to reap some rewards. Students from the UCA went with Dr Castillo to Rome to negotiate the leadership of the university and succeeded in having the Rector removed.

Despite the fact that she carried and gave birth to her daughter, worked hard for the FSLN, was once expelled from the university (along with a hundred others) and was expected to sign a 'good girl' declaration (which she didn't) in order to be allowed to resume classes, Nora continued to study and to get good marks, even from the Somocista judges. She successfully graduated in Law in 1971.

Jorgé had the offer of a scholarship to study anthropology in Italy for a year, and Nora was keen to accompany him. Her father, still devoted to his firstborn, helped her financially so that she could study banking law and computer programming while she was there. So Nora got her trip to Europe after all and became quite fluent in Italian. They lived in Pavia, not far from Milan, where Nora could take advantage of the rich cultural life that Italy had to offer. Jorgé studied in Pavia and Nora at the University of the Sacred Heart (another Catholic institution!) in Milan itself. This was really a year out for them, away from oppression and the student struggle. They didn't return until the middle of 1973.

This meant that they were not personally affected by the earthquake which destroyed Managua on the 23rd of December 1972, around midnight...

Uriel Molina, who was leading a three-day fast in the Managua cathedral by the student Christian community remembers the first, violent tremor, 'We all ran out in panic, not before all the books in the library fell on me, like an air raid.' (1) Then as Tomás Borge stood still in suspense as the aftershocks continued - a black cat shot by, he said, fleeing the God of Wrath. The second shudder followed shortly after the first. The shock, the crack, as if the earthquake happens inside you, or - as Gioconda Belli puts it - 'the hoarse groaning in the very depths of our roots'. (2)

The centre of the city was devastated - 10,000 people died,20,000 were wounded and 30,000 lost their homes. The wooden houses in the poor *barrios* simply collapsed. Fortunately not many people were hurt there. It was those in smart town houses built of stone that were buried beneath the rubble. The beautiful cathedral was an empty shell.

The mass exodus began on Christmas Eve, with the unending column of refugees who were moving out, dazed but in little panic. Within a few days the stench from corpses in the tropical heat was described as overpowering and the government had to suspend food distribution in the city centre in order to compel the evacuation of stragglers, due to the serious health risks (3)

45

The international press reported that, 'Managua is finished. It is a city with no water supply, no local telephone service, no electrical power.'(4) Photographs showed looters in the shattered streets. (5) By December 28th troops had sealed off Managua and United States Army engineers, from the Panama Canal Zone, moved in with bulldozers and earth movers to clear the smouldering rubble.

Ironically as the reports of the situation in Managua came through, they were accompanied on the same pages by reports of the pre-Christmas United States air raid bombings of Hanoi city. One photograph, of the demolished railway station, looked exactly like those coming out of Managua.

After the earthquake the Christian groups threw themselves into doing humanitarian work in the *barrios*. It was a way of helping the homeless but it was also a way of organising. The community became a centre for political activity. The Christian Movement for Revolution began working in eight *barrios*, carrying out investigations into main problems - water, electricity, health. The idea was that community organisations would begin to deal with the problems. 'The whole Christian movement was now being oriented in one way or other by the Front... people working in the popular movements were recruited into the Front... We were still protected by the mantle of Christianity and could operate more openly, that's one reason the movement was so important,' explained Luis Carrión. (6)

Somoza's response to the disaster certainly contributed to his final downfall. After news of the earthquake had flashed around the world, an international relief fund was set up and money came pouring in. Or so the newspapers said. But there was no mention of a housing reconstruction programme, nor about provision for orphans, nor extended health care. Instead, after bulldozers had cleared the centre of the city, workmen started to replace the pavements with beautiful large hexagonal cobble stones. Since the original commercial zone in the north of the city had been destroyed, Somoza decided to build three others, in the east, west and south. He also personally bought up several more companies that year. (He already owned hundreds.) 'It was outrageous,' says Rosario Murillo, a friend of Nora's from school, who had lost her baby son in the earthquake. 'People were angry and bitter. That earthquake led to a consensus that Somoza had to be got rid of and that time was near.' (7) Out of the despair and chaos, people's anger rose.

It was the building workers who went on strike first, in 1973. The students organised themselves in support. The teachers, health workers and factory workers came out on strike too. Only a few buses carried on running. There was a quiet over Managua, ominous and heavy as the dry season got drier and the heat grew hotter.

Workers sat outside on the hexagonal paving stones, with their placards, shielding themselves from the sun with a newspaper or handkerchief, or, if they were lucky, taking advantage of a shady tree.

The National Guard were everywhere, keeping watch, but keeping silent too. It was at this stage that Nora returned to Managua with Jorgé and little Muriel. In July 1973, after some months of planning, students all over the country demonstrated in support of the workers. It was a massive action.

On September 17th 1973, the National Guard raided a safe house in Nandaime and captured Nora's comrade Oscar Turcios, along with Ricardo Morales. They were severely tortured and their mutilated bodies were then dumped out of the town on a lonely road, to be discovered the following day. 'They tried to say Oscar was killed in a jeep wreck, but it was cold blooded murder,' Nora told *The Washington Post* later. (8)

To lose two leaders was a great loss for the FSLN and for Nora, this must also have been a deep personal loss. Oscar Turcios had been her chief and her mentor and he had been her friend, too, for four years. 'Without wanting to idealise him - he had his faults like anyone else - I'll always remember Oscar with a great deal of love,' she said. (9) For a while Nora was so affected by the circumstances of this death, that she left her political

47

life behind and 'burrowed into her family, becoming more dependent on her husband.' (10)

However, the apprenticeship she had served with Oscar Turcios was only a beginning for Nora; she went on to become a leader in the FSLN, a rôle model to inspire thousands of young people to join the struggle, a hero in the end.

Nora started work for one of the largest construction companies in Nicaragua, SOVIPE. She was both lawyer and head of personnel for the firm. Young women like Nora and her friends were for the first time entering the professions and having to cope with the ingrained sexism they found there. Gioconda Belli, who went into advertising, the first woman publicist in Nicaragua, describes the need for an attractive young woman to prove herself as professionally competent. (11) Milú Vargas, who went into her father's law firm, says: 'I was the only woman lawyer there. Of course, I began to notice the sexism that was simply habitual among the men. Even on the part of the male clients: they tended to treat me as a sex object, while they treated the other lawyers as equals.'

For Nora, the even more macho preserve of the construction industry caused similar problems. However, she did enjoy some of the work she was doing, and remembered, 'when I was a lawyer what I liked most was the negotiating part of the job, making contracts.' Although she was modest about her own achievements, Nora was always a fluent speaker: 'She has the ability to speak with an uncommon fluidity and orderliness,' remarked Margaret Randall who interviewed Nora in 1980 and, in 1987, the *Envio* interviewers described her as 'bringing up memories that flowed out of each other and formed their own pattern.'

As a young woman involved in the revolutionary movement, Nora was leading a dangerous double life. 'The job gave me a cloak, a very good cover. It allowed me to move in government circles. I had contact with ministers of state and, to a certain extent, with members of the National

48

Guard.' (12) At home, Nora did not need to cover up her political leanings since her own husband was a militant.

In contrast, Gioconda Belli would lock herself in the bathroom to read FSLN documents which she kept hidden from her husband behind a plaster board panel in the false ceiling. Even more serious, Milú Vargas' husband was a minister in Somoza's government and later became a lieutenant colonel in the army.

Nora certainly had to keep up the image of a respectable middle class Liberal with her own parents and in the family social circles, as well as professionally. Because of the FSLN security measures, you would never be quite sure who was involved in the organisation. Whether at work or attending social functions you might or might not be mingling with other collaborators. Who else was in the secret? You always had to be careful. However, in the case of Somoza's henchmen, his allies and the chiefs of the National Guard, you were usually quite clear about whether or not you were talking to a monster; they were much more open about their activities.

It may seem extraordinary that the state security didn't uncover more of the collaborators. In some senses this reflects the arrogance and stupidity of a corrupt régime led by a sadist who believed he could get away with anything. But it also reflects the class image of the established Nicaraguan bourgeoisie, who for so long had tolerated the dictatorship and to whose gracious way of life those coarse henchmen aspired.

The régime had a very class oriented view of revolution. As Gioconda Belli explains in her novel *La Mujer Habitada*, aristocrats were really above suspicion and even the opposition leaders were not under surveillance. (13) Perhaps especially the traditional view of women as appendages, not operating according to their own beliefs, meant that it was very difficult to conceive of a young middle class woman, probably married, with one or two small children, as having any political involvement. The FSLN certainly seemed to take full advantage of this capacity of women collaborators to move freely in the highest circles, gain audience, travel and speak publicly abroad about the Nicaraguan reality.

49

Gioconda Belli discusses this kind of paradox for women like herself and Nora through Lavinia, the central character in her novel: 'Since she had been in the movement, trying to assimilate the idea of abandoning the status quo, to change herself into a different kind of person, transcend that individual life constrained by its origins, she had been longing for the moment when she could participate more actively... (However) apparently the only thing she could do to serve the movement was to play the rôle of her own life!'(14)

There must have been many occasions when Nora had to attend events that she didn't want to and behave courteously to people she abhorred. How could she forget what they really were? For example, Tomás Borge had been arrested by the Guard after leaving a secret meeting in Colonia Centro America on February 4th 1976, and tortured along with thirteen other comrades. They were being held in the dungeons of the National Palace. She might be talking to the general who had authorised their torture.

During 1975, the FSLN went through serious internal problems. The leadership split into three so-called 'tendencies': the Proletariat Tendency, the Prolonged Popular War Tendency and the Insurrectionist Tendency.

The Proletariat Tendency wanted to establish an orthodox Marxist party and to concentrate on organisational work among the urban working class, to provide the social base for a revolutionary movement.

Tomás Borge, Henri Ruiz and Bayardo Arce, one of Jorgé's student comrades, formed the Prolonged Popular War Tendency which insisted on the rural campaign of attrition against the Guard on the model of Vietnam. Tomás Borge also tried to enlist the help of the priests.

The Insurrectionists, led by the Ortega brothers, (Camilo, Humberto and Daniel) wanted to form a multi-class alliance and believed in the potential to overthrow the régime. They carried out insurrections in various cities across the country and also planned a provisional government.

Nora said, 'When the FSLN split into three tendencies my participation diminished quite a bit and I became isolated from the political struggle. I didn't want to take sides in the split so my involvement was reduced almost exclusively to giving financial aid to the tendencies.' The political split mirrored other kinds of divisions in her life and she added, 'to be completely honest, there were personal reasons as well for my poor showing at that time.' (15)

Nora's married life had not turned out the way she had hoped. Jorgé had agreed, in principle, that her political life would come first, ' but it didn't work out that way in practice.' Although men may have welcomed the collaboration of women as comrades it seems that many of them didn't welcome the political involvement of a woman with whom they had an intimate relationship. In *La Mujer Habitada*, Gioconda Belli depicts this reluctance clearly, on the part of the main character, Lavinia's lover, Felipe. In some cases this may be explained by the felt male need to protect his mate; but there is the alternate explanation that what men jealously guarded was not their woman but their own rôle in the revolution, the action and the excitement.

Moreover, 'men don't like competence in a woman, they don't want her to go forward,' says Guadelupe.

Nora had sought a revolutionary relationship between man and woman but had come up against the prejudices of the past, the expectations of what a wife and mother should be and do, supporting her man, a beautiful face, the Madonna with child, waiting calmly alone at home, keeping the dinner warm, keeping the bed warm, while her hero was out courting danger in clandestine operations she was not allowed to know of.

Guadelupe recalled, 'Of course, at first, Jorgé was madly in love with her - like everyone was! - but after a while he began to want to control everything she did. She wasn't even allowed to pay if they went out to eat.'

There must have been a great deal of conflict on the surface and a lot of hurt underneath. Nora describes it as 'an unhealthy, destructive type of relationship' which undermined her self-esteem, her belief in herself. Her

51

attempts to make the relationship work led to constant disappointment when she found Jorgé was neither willing nor able to meet her at the same level of integrity.

As she put it, 'A man still hasn't overcome his fear of his wife having her own life and still isn't ready to accept what I call a 'woman individual', who has responsibilities outside the home. On the other hand, women are no longer disposed to stay within the four walls of their home. That's why there have been so many divorces, so many problems between couples, with the revolution.'

But most of all, when she looked back at this phase, Nora remembered how her marriage hindered her involvement in the revolutionary movement. 'Can you understand that kind of conflict,' she asked Margaret Randall during an interview, 'where personal problems get a stranglehold on your life? You have lots of good intentions but the way you lead your life doesn't allow you to act on them. It wasn't until I made a complete break with that relationship that I was really able to devote myself to the struggle.'

In 1976 Nora and Jorgé separated, but not before another daughter was born, baby Dafne (maybe the result of an attempt at reconciliation?). Jorgé left Nicaragua for Mexico, where some of the FSLN leaders were based.

At first the separation was very hard for Nora. In the same interview she said, 'when I first left my husband, I thought the world was going to fall apart.' But later she recorded, 'once again I began to challenge myself: am I giving what I ought to give and doing what I ought to do? or am I simply trying to soothe my conscience with small things where I risk little or where I risk absolutely nothing?'

Because of the problems in her marriage, Nora had, in many ways, reverted to type: she was living a pleasant bourgeois life as a company executive with a good position and a good income. 'Am I going to conform,' she asked herself, 'by settling down into a comfortable, peaceful life, with money, house, car, just a friendly, agreeable, intelligent woman?'

52

At this time Nora was living in a comfortable house in a respectable middle class Managua neighbourhood called Altamira, with her two children and a young woman who looked after them while Nora was at work. She also had a lodger, María Elena Corzo Corea, who had studied administration at the UCA and then, like Nora, followed postgraduate studies in Italy, in real estate. They were now professional colleagues, María working as an executive for Provinsa, a subsidiary company of SOVIPE.

Nora's parents, who had moved out of Managua after the earthquake, had to accept the fact of the break-up of Nora's marriage. Doña Muriel's attitude now (at least) reflects a somewhat surprising admiration for her daughter's independence: 'she was a professional, earning good money; she didn't need a husband.' We can imagine her turning Nora's father Segundo round to this viewpoint.

Nora's Christian conscience came to the fore against this slide into materialism. She also began to think of those she had known in the struggle and who had died - like Oscar Turcios and Ricardo Morales. It wasn't possible that others were struggling and she did nothing. The death of Carlos Fonseca at around this time also affected her deeply.

Carlos Fonseca was the undisputed leader of the FSLN. He had returned to Nicaragua at the end of the previous year to try and settle the dispute between the three tendencies. The comrades believed that due to his intervention all their problems had ended and the FSLN had been saved.(17)

He was killed in a confrontation with the Guard in the mountains near Zinica (November 8th 1976). Nora said, 'I only saw him once but he was always present. For us the lifelines, the examples, the political teachings, came from Carlos.' For much of the life of the FSLN, Carlos Fonseca had been outside the country. 'We didn't see him, but he had an enormous presence.' He had written some documents, but more than anything, 'what was his came to us through the oral tradition.'

Nora's old friend Carlos Agüero travelled with Fonseca on his clandestine journey through the country and was there when he died. He was killed in an ambush and later his body was found by the Guard, sprawled against the trunk of a tree. 'His eyes remained open, and always will, seeing beyond life and death.' One comrade in Managua told Carlos Nuñez calmly, when he said that the news was true: 'No, it's just another lie of those sons-of- bitches. Carlos Fonseca cannot die.'(18)

While his loss was great, Carlos Fonseca remained present like all the other heroes and martyrs of the revolution. Banners would bear the slogan: *Carlos, presente!*

The Nicaraguan revolution is a history of collective struggle... 'if you forget this, you can't keep moving forward... People criticise us,' said Nora shortly before her own death, 'saying the Sandinistas have a death cult, but the dead are part of us, are our living force, they accompany us and help us. I think Christians can understand this very well.'

Therefore, Nora decided: no more excuses. She made the leap of revolutionary faith and became more involved in the FSLN.

One of Nora's first major achievements, within this context, was the foundation of a women's political organisation. Peasant women were already organised; the Organisation of Democratic Women was allied to the Nicaraguan Socialist Party (to which many people belonged before joining up with the FSLN) and the International Democratic Women's Organisation. Doris Tijerino and Gladys Báez were involved in setting up the (FSLN) Patriotic Alliance of Nicaraguan Women in the sixties, which raised money for the revolution and agitated for better conditions in hospitals.

Nora first met Lea Guido in 1974 at the house of a friend they had in common, Yolanda Huembes, during a children's birthday party. Lea was lecturing in Sociology at the UNAN, having recently returned from studying in Switzerland, and was very advanced in her political analysis, according to Guadelupe Salinas. Her background was unusual in that her father had paid for excellent private schools in Europe while her mother still sold meat in the Mercado Oriental of Managua. Maybe something similar in the contradictions of both their lives as well as a similar desire for putting ideas into practice meant that the two women quickly developed a close friendship.

'We immediately became sisters,' Lea said at Nora's funeral. (19) Later she explained: 'It wasn't just that we were both in the FSLN and had political sympathies, it was also a friendship between women. And all that continued even though we then went off and followed different tendencies - I was in the Proletariat Tendency with Jaime Wheelock, Nora was with the Insurrectionists. We worked together closely between 1975 and 1978.'(20)

It was Lea, Nora and Gloria Carrión who got the women's group going. It was purportedly Jaimé Wheelock who suggested a work commission to look at women's problems and work towards the creation of a broad-based women's association. (21) Maybe the suggestion coincided with what some of the women collaborators were also thinking: 'it was a women's initiative within the FSLN,' says Guadelupe.

Gloria was the younger sister of Luis Carrión: she had recently returned from abroad, having studied Education in the United States and her commitment to the struggle had been strengthened by her brother going underground. Lea contacted Milú Vargas to ask if she wanted to join them. 'For the first time I was able to talk to other women about what I was feeling, other women who shared my politics and who were experiencing the same kind of discrimination.' says Milú. (22)

According to Lea Guido, Nora played an important rôle in the organisation, particularly through her participation in meetings discussing the direction the organisation should take. They used to meet at Nora's house. 'Our goal was to get women to participate more actively in the solution to our country's social and economic problems. I remember us spending a whole night (at Nora's little house in Altamira) trying to decide on a name that would reflect this idea.' Lea told Margaret Randall.(23)

The Association of Women confronting the Nation's Problems (AMPRONAC) was launched on September 29th 1977, nine days after the lifting of the state of siege, in the Church of Las Palmas in Managua; this first national assembly was reported internationally. The group denounced the human rights violations 'which have taken on alarming dimensions, as affirmed by religious organisations such as the Nicaraguan Conference of Bishops... and by international organisations like Amnesty...' (24).

One of the first tasks was to investigate and improve the situation of women prisoners. Peasant women from the north came to speak about the repression in the mountains and the mass murders being carried out there - at great personal risk since giving testimony meant exposing themselves publicly.

Initially the Association involved mainly bourgeois women, whose participation was particularly valuable because they could get to see government officials, have interviews with, for instance, the head of Public Relations of the National Guard without fear of being arrested, and use international forums to denounce what was happening in Nicaragua. However, few of the women wanted to be publicly identified as members of the association - and in one sense this was pragmatic since it would probably have curtailed their lobbying activities.

In Nora's case, identification would have excluded her from taking part in an up-coming military operation and Gloria ran a nursery school which served as a cover for an important propaganda system. So neither of these women were public figures of AMPRONAC although they were involved from the beginning. Only these three were members of the FSLN at the time - and Lea was the only one publicly identified with both organisations.

The Association quickly began to involve a much wider range of women. 'We had many, many women who weren't going to participate in the struggle unless we could provide ways for them to organise *as women.*' (25)

Nora emphasised that Nicaraguan women have never been apathetic. 'In spite of the fact that we haven't always participated in the front lines, we were always concerned about what was going on. And there is another thing: women here love their children like a passion. Our women are very demonstrative, very committed.' (26) The women were committed to bringing down the dictatorship: thus began a tradition of revolutionary motherhood.

AMPRONAC was phenomenally successful. From 60 women at its first assembly, it grew to over 8000 in the final days of the insurrection. It organised demonstrations, occupied churches, circulated petitions, carried messages from political prisoners to their families and lobbied the government to find out the whereabouts of 'the disappeared.' (27)

'I remember how the women were shy at first,' Nora recalled. 'They'd tell us "OK I'm willing to work in my neighbourhood, but just for water and electricity and things like that." But with a bit more effort - we didn't have to make such an enormous effort - those women began taking part on an ever more solid basis... Those women saw what was going on and they wanted to confront things and change them. Once they got involved they began to grow.' (28)

Nora's contribution was that of organising women and mothers for the freedom of their family and their own emancipation, summarised Sofía Montenegro in her obituary.

Analysts have pointed out that in Nicaragua much of the revolutionary activity took place in the reproductive, rather than the productive, sphere - at the neighbourhood level rather than in factories or other workplaces. The strategy of 'a people in arms' that was so essential to the Sandinista victory over the dictator depended on the mobilisation of entire communities and that means - though it is not always stated as such - on the massive participation of women, as the population was organised, *barrio* by *barrio*. (29)

In 1986 Nora recalled saying to Margaret Randall, 'Don't write about those whom we've made famous. Write about the women who hid the contact bombs in their skirts and fooled the guards with their cunning. The majority of women participated like this and that's how we made the revolution, with women.'

International Women's Day

From 1976 Somoza's popularity hit an all time low. There was an increasing realisation that he could not keep getting away with this level of oppression for very much longer. Even the bourgeoisie were repelled by the atrocities of the régime and the bad taste of the *nouveau riche*. The feeling, at home and abroad, was that pretty soon he would have to resign. Despite Somoza's loss of popularity, the United States continued to support him. Several United States military advisers were in the country, training the National Guard in the sort of psychological warfare developed by the CIA, and practised elsewhere, such as Vietnam. As a result it was not uncommon for the women of whole villages in the countryside to be subjected to organised rape by the National Guard, and women who were arrested were systematically raped and tortured. (1)

'Aid' projects such as the Institute for Peasant Welfare, which received a loan of US$14 million, targeted zones of major guerrilla activities and were used as a cover for counter-insurgency attacks. The Aid Director for Nicaragua had supervised similar projects in Vietnam ten years previously. (2)

One of the locally recruited agents of the CIA was General Peréz Vega, nicknamed *El Perro* (The Dog) because of his appalling and bestial behaviour. He was Somoza's right hand man, in charge of the 'clean-up' operations in the north. He had overseen the massacre at El Cuá in the early seventies.

El Cuá is a village in the north of Nicaragua that was a strategic base used by the Government forces to counter the revolution. It was a concentration camp. The Guard brought people there, gagged and blindfold, from all over the Northern countryside. The prisoners were mainly peasants, in fact anyone they thought might have anything to do with the Sandinistas - men, women, children and old people. The soldiers, under the command of *El Perro* went out and burned down farms, burning people alive. They set dogs to sniff out revolutionaries and the women were

59

raped to find out where the *guerrilleros* were hiding. The men were kept in underground dungeons and tortured there. Peasants were taken up in helicopters and thrown out alive. Mass graves were dug and filled up out among the maize fields. El Cuá. Its very name was a nightmare. (3)

Around this time Nora's marriage to Jorgé came to a definitive end. He had not contested the divorce and, as Nora received the *decree nisi*, the opportunity arose for her to demonstrate her new level of commitment to the revolution. *El Perro* showed an interest in developing some land next to a real estate initiative of the construction company that Nora worked for. She remembered *El Perro* clearly: ' he was the worst kind of torturer. Any adjective I could use to describe him would be pale in comparison with the reality of his crimes.' (4) When she met this 'worst sort of animal' through work, he quickly developed a passionate interest in her.

Nora passed on the news of her repellent admirer: 'I told the Organisation I was in a good position to get closer to The Dog. We knew we could take advantage of the situation to get information from the guy. The comrades told me to keep the relationship going but not to push it any further for the moment.'

'When I went to see him (*El Perro*) at his office I would play my rôle to the letter. I had to take the utmost care - be cordial and cool at one and the same time. Being pleasant to that man was one of the most difficult things I have ever been called on to do.'

Nora's contact in the FSLN was one of the few full-time members, José María Alvarado, whose *nombre de guerra* was Chester. He had been a member of the FSLN since the 1960s, as a collaborator ('life expectancy then for a full-blown member was said to be 72 hours!') and had gone underground in 1975. He belonged to the Insurrectionist Tendency, working closely with Camilo Ortega who was in charge of the internal resistance. Chester described himself as Camilo Ortega's right-hand man.

It was Camilo who first suggested Chester become Nora's contact, because, like her, he was exceptionally tall, skinny and white. If Nora were to keep meeting up with a short dark-skinned peasant, she might attract attention. Chester was also from the middle classes and, in fact, knew Nora distantly through other families in Granada, although he was eight years older than her: 'I had probably met her last when she was ten and I was eighteen.'

However, the first time they made contact as revolutionaries, neither of them knew who they were going to meet. Nora was now operating under the warname Angela and he was Chester. The rendezvous that was set up for them was an expensive bar-restaurant *El Esquimo* which sells ice creams and steaks. Instead of a password, Chester was to offer Angela a light with a red cigarette lighter. When he walked in, he saw Nora waiting and they 'sort of recognised each other.' Chester realised it must be Nora he was supposed to meet and sat down next to her.

'She ordered an ice-cream and I ordered a coffee. We began to chat, we laughed a lot, she was always a real clown and I like clowning too. I thought she was chatting me up, afterwards she told me she thought I was chatting her up... But she was nervous, she kept telling me: actually I'm meeting someone. She was obviously anxious that I might identify her contact. I said: that's okay - when he turns up, I'll leave... In the end I put her out of her misery. When she got out yet another cigarette, I flourished the red lighter and she gave me a look as if to say: You bastard! Even when we went out to the car, she was very tense. Of course, I'd had a lot of experience of clandestine activity, she was still quite new to it...'

Thus, a time of even deeper 'conspiracy' for Nora began. As well as maintaining her cover as a respectable bourgeois professional, she was also required to employ her female charms to ensnare *El Perro*, a man whom she abhorred, in order to further the aims of the revolution. Can it be called a revolutionary act?

Nora somehow managed to keep him at arm's length for over a year. 'The guy had a reputation for being a womaniser and, like a classic member of the Guard, he went after the women he fancied, by good or bad

61

means, however and whenever he felt like it.' He was renowned for getting women to give themselves to him in return for a favour of some kind, for example if they wanted to help a relative in prison.

As Nora put it, when PÈrez Vega found out that Nora's divorce had come through, he said to himself, like a classic macho, 'That woman is easy prey now' and he began an all-out campaign to get her into bed.

Nora told Chester that this was a good time to get what they wanted from *El Perro*. She was told 'to keep him interested' until they had analysed the situation. The 'planning committee' included Daniel Ortega, who was in Honduras, Victor Manuel Tirado and Henri Ruiz. Nora was left to walk the tightrope, 'I had to keep him thinking I would give in and at the same time to hold back until the time was right.' This ambivalence kept him interested for a while but there came a point when it was impossible to keep him dangling any more. 'Either I had to give in or we'd lose our chance.'

However, the Insurrectionist Tendency were at that time absorbed with planning an attempt at an all-out uprising - which eventually failed because it wasn't sufficiently co-ordinated. A small group of militants, mainly from the community on Solentiname, the peasants and fisherfolk mobilised by Father Ernesto Cardenal, attacked the barracks at San Carlos on October 13th 1977. But the attack was a failure and the force had to flee. There was also heavy fighting in Masaya where the FSLN managed to close the Masaya-Tipitapa road. Unfortunately, members of the Prolonged Popular War Tendency got in the way. They walked into the ambush because nobody had told them what was going on and one of their commanders, codename Frederico, was killed.

Despite the blunders, it was 'the October Offensive' that convinced a lot of people it was possible to take on the Guard and the following month, a moderate group of professional people calling themselves The Twelve made an announcement in *La Prensa* that they supported the FSLN. The group included the writer Sergio Ramírez, two priests, Father Miguel d'Escoto and Fernando Cardenal, and the banker, Arturo Cruz. They were based in Costa Rica along with Humberto Ortega. Their support succeeded in removing the extremist image that the Front had had so far. (5)

It was against this background, with forces pushing Nicaragua inevitably towards change, that Nora got the opportunity to carry out the action that made her so famous and earned for her 'a permanent niche in the Sandinista pantheon of heroes'. (6)

She too was inexorably moving towards a more radical political position. At the beginning of 1978 an event occurred which had enormous importance for her - the assassination of Pedro Chamorro, the conservative opposition leader and editor of the anti-Somocista newspaper, *La Prensa*. It was generally believed that the assassination had been ordered by Somoza's son and heir, Antonio, in an attempt to discourage the right-wing opposition. This strategy seriously backfired on the dictator, since the action was universally condemned. Even the Carter régime in the United States suggested it would be better for Somoza to leave and said that the United States would be prepared to recognise a provisional government to replace him. (7)

The statement from AMPRONAC, written as soon as the news about Pedro's death was heard on the morning of 10th January and later printed in *La Prensa*, was one of many statements from a range of Nicaraguan organisations: 'We condemn the cowardly crime against Dr Chamorro who has added his blood to that of the Nicaraguan people. For denouncing crimes against the people through the wide circulation of *La Prensa*, the director has now been added to the list of victims. We renew our call for all sectors of society to join forces to eradicate the system which is responsible for crimes and violence which the Nicaraguan people suffer daily.'(8)

The day following the assassination, Managua came to a standstill. Chamorro's body was carried from the Hospital Oriental to his home - a journey of ten kilometres - accompanied by a crowd of around 50,000 people: 'the multitude, in a spontaneous gesture of solidarity and respect for a brave and honest man, walked a long and difficult path, like the one which Pedro Joaquín followed all his life and which the whole of Nicaragua needs to follow in pursuit of real freedom.' (9) AMPRONAC was at the head of the demonstration with their banner. Those who were unable to take part in the protest march sat listening to the commentary on their radios. A twelve day national strike was called by the Nicaraguan Chamber of Commerce, which urged all places of business to close their doors on the day of the funeral .

A commission from AMPRONAC visited the Chamorro house to offer condolences to the widow Violeta and her children. But Nora said, 'It wasn't Pedro's death itself - although I knew him. What affected me was seeing people take to the streets and feeling that this was not the way we were going to be able to overthrow the dictatorship. I was stuck in traffic that day in *barrio* El Dorado. It was one of those moments when suddenly the coconut breaks open... like a revelation when you suddenly understand... I finally understood that armed struggle was the only solution, that you can't hold up a flower against a rifle, that we were in the streets but that if this force didn't get organised, we wouldn't achieve much. For me it was a moment of conviction: either I took up arms and made a total commitment or nothing was going to change.'

It had taken eleven years since that first protest march supporting Agüero, where people's hopes had been trampled on so tragically, for Nora to shift her philosophical and moral perspective to one which contained the reality of armed resistance and insurrection.

Women everywhere were beginning to organise. AMPRONAC played an active rôle in planning the occupation of the United Nations offices by the families of the disappeared and political prisoners, which coincided with the strike on the day of Chamorro's funeral. Women pickets took part in the occupation.

On 30th January a meeting of 600 women from all walks of life, demonstrating in support of the occupation, was broken up by the Guard using tear gas and assault. But 'because of the repression, we had established a series of practical measures to defend our activities. We would provide handkerchiefs soaked in lemonade and bicarbonate of soda to protect ourselves against the effects of tear gas.' (10)

Unlike the bourgeoisie who only demanded justice for Chamorro's case, AMPRONAC's slogan was: 'Where are our peasant brothers and sisters? Let the assassins respond!' (11) Clashes between demonstrators and the National Guard were the cause of many deaths around the country.

By that time, the comrades had a plan, which was to kidnap General Vega and exchange him for information and political prisoners. Nora was to invite the General to her house on a prearranged day and disarm him (both metaphorically and literally). Three comrades would be hidden in the house and when Nora gave the signal, they would move into action.

It seems clear that the basic idea behind 'Operation *El Perro'* was Nora's. It was the physical attraction that the General felt for her that provided the opportunity for the FSLN to get close to him and use him. It must have been the case that, to a limited extent, attractive middle class women were regularly used by the FSLN as sexual objects, as bait, in the social rôle they played as conspirators against the dictatorship, wining and dining with the upper echelons of the enemy. Similarly, working class and peasant women would use the power of their sexuality to fool the ordinary soldiers as they smuggled messages and bombs past them.

However, this is the only (documented) major operation that hinges on this relationship. Perhaps what made it the more surprising, was that Nora, like so many other women, had become involved in the revolutionary movement in order to discover a new identity for woman. She had dissolved her own marriage because it did not live up to the aspirations that she had and yet at the same time she was prepared to play a game of seduction she despised in order to further the revolution. However, she had already explored this possibility with Guadelupe and other student friends - the Mata Hari rôle.

The Ortegas wished to take advantage of the opportunity. However, Nora remembers that the planning committee gave her the final choice as to whether the action would go forward. 'The comrades made it clear that I would not be able to return to my life, I couldn't go back to my daughters. They told me I would bear the brunt of all kinds of misconceptions and suspicions about what I had done. From the beginning I knew I would have to go underground. And no-one knew then that the triumph would come so soon.' This was not to mention the personal danger she might run in the operation. After all she was going to seduce a rapist.

They gave her time to think about it. It was a difficult decision. The idea of leaving her daughters was the worst part. Muriel was then aged six and little Dafne only two. 'It was the thought of leaving them, being separated from them that cost me the most.'

But as with many women fighting, it was the thought of her children's future that made her decide. 'I wanted to bring about a better world for them and other children.' Presumably she believed that the children themselves would not be in any real danger because of her actions...

The plans for Operation *El Perro* continued to be postponed because the Ortegas wanted to take advantage of the national strike. At the beginning of February the FSLN attacked Rivas and Granada. It was Camilo Ortega who led the attack on the National Guard garrison in Granada. But this military action failed to have maximum effect because of poor communications between Managua and San José. As Chester described it, 'we were sitting, 28 men in a tiny house, lots of tension, waiting through the night for the people who were supposed to have turned up from Costa Rica the previous night. When we got in touch with Humberto, he said: No, they're coming back..'

In the middle of February, a month after Chamorro's funeral, a mass in his honour was held in Monimbó, the Indian quarter of Masaya. The Guard burst in and sprayed tear gas on the congregation. Coughing, crying, confused, the Indians scattered to their homes. During the night

66

they built barricades and trenches. The first popular uprising against Somoza began. The Indian women were in the thick of the battle. The courage of the Indian community was made famous by the song of Carlos Mejía Godoy: 'You will live on, Monimbó, the pure flame of the people; I hear your heart, the warrior's drum beat. Where the Indian fell fighting, that's where the granadilla tree grows - from which we can make the *marimba* to play the sounds of freedom'. (12)

That night *El Perro* sent the fighter planes over Masaya. The night sky was on fire at the horizon. Even from the capital the bombs could be heard exploding. The children slept oblivious to the evil of the world. In Monimbó, people were running, running, down the alleyways, away from the fire, or caught by the General's men.

Then, on February 26th, Camilo Ortega, who had gone to Masaya with reinforcements for the uprising, was captured as an infiltrator and assassinated by the National Guard. 'I communicated with Humberto that same night,' recalls Chester. 'Remember, there were only seven of us full-time. I told him someone from the National Directorate had to come and support us in Operation *El Perro*... Nora couldn't keep on giving excuses....'

Hilario Sánchez was sent to be head of the commando, with the message that, 'We're not very convinced this is a good idea,' and the plan was finally put into action.

After the kidnapping, Nora was to go to Costa Rica. She arranged for a cousin, who was married to a North American, to look after her daughters for a while and she left them there shortly before the action. She believed they would be safer there, given the repression that was sure to follow. 'There was a real danger for her daughters,' confirms Chester. 'The Guard were quite capable of bursting into the house and taking them away.'

Nora was unable to confide in any of her friends. 'I suspected something was going to happen,' says Lea Guido, 'because Nora had asked me to get hold of a list of political prisoners - and that was common if there was going to be some kind of operation.' (13)

The day chosen was March 8th, International Women's Day. We can imagine this was a coincidence, although it has obvious resonance for the emancipation of women. AMPRONAC celebrated Nicaraguan Women's Week, in the early days of March, launching an appeal with demands for an end to repression for all and the end of discrimination against women. Their call pointed to the need for women to join the struggle for a free country.(14) On the 8th March *La Prensa* carried a photograph of women weeping: 'on women's day we mustn't forget the wives and mothers of disappeared *campesinos*.'

Nora had already fobbed off *El Perro* for the last time, with her budding diplomat's skills, saying, that 'as an independent woman, she had the right to choose who, where and when.' He had accepted the offer with alacrity.

However, the best laid plans do not always work out. When Nora rang his office at 4 o'clock in the afternoon, *El Perro* was out of town. She left an urgent message with his secretary and within 45 minutes the General called to say he would be right over. Nora dashed out to the supermarket to get a bottle of whisky. Soon after she got back, the General turned up.

Thus began an event which was surreal, unreal, as Nora looked back to see herself in her own house as if in a film, a farce: 'I laugh when I think of it now... even then it seemed a bit funny... although of course I wasn't laughing at the time.' She remembered the General's approach was very direct. He had no time for a drink or a chat, none of the usual subtleties or delicacy. He arrived and said: 'Let's get on with it' and they went right to the bedroom. Here everything went according to plan. They undressed and Nora disarmed *El Perro*. 'The General undoubtedly thought he was in for a special night: he was. At that moment Astorga's accomplices jumped out of hiding and slit Perez' throat from ear to ear,' was how *Time Magazine* described the incident to the United States. (15)

According to Nora, and this is corroborated by Chester, the comrades burst in and General Vega put up a great deal of resistance. Nora was sent to get rid of the driver/bodyguard, using the pretext that the General wanted some *ron plata* (a working class brand of rum which the General was not likely to stock in the bar of his limousine). Then she went to the garage to get the car out. When she returned the comrades (Hilario Sánchez, Arnaldo Quant and Moisés Riviera) came out and told her they had had to kill him. 'He was about 45 or 50 but he was very strong. He put up too heavy a fight,' Nora told Margaret Randall. This was despite the fact he had been administered with a dose of anaesthetic, Promisol, and tied up! The legend is that the body was left in Nora's bedroom, draped in a black and red Sandinista flag. (17)

They had to move quickly. Nora recounted how she dropped off the comrades at the spot where they were to be picked up by another driver and then returned the car to its owner 'who, needless to say, didn't know what it had been used for.'

But Chester's account has a rather more hurried feel to it. 'For the record, we never planned to assassinate the guy. And I had to get Nora out of there. I drove her down to the Costa Rican border - we were in a Volvo, maybe an Audi - there should have been someone waiting there, but there wasn't. I couldn't leave her there. I said: I'll take you to the other end of the corridor.'

Chester knew the border well as he had fought with Eden Pastora at Cardenas in the October 1977 offensive. But, 'there was no-one there either. I communicated with Humberto and early the following day they sent someone, a *compañera* called Amanda. Nora was rather conspicuous, she was dressed all in white and had no other clothes, she had nothing with her. So Amanda had to swap shirts with her. There was no way that they could swap trousers, Nora was too tall and had very slim hips, Amanda was a small woman. The shirt was a bit tight but it wasn't bad. So off she went to the Southern Front...'

As he was driving back, Chester put on the radio, but there was no news of the assassination. 'I went up to Altamira and walked by Nora's house. There were a lot of people around. I asked: What happened?'

The FSLN had called the General's wife during the night and Security Police broke down the doors at 8am the following morning. At first the government declined to comment on the claim made by the FSLN over the radio that 'Vega was slain because he resisted capture.' Police Chief Colonel Alesio Gutierrez announced that the general's body had not been removed from the Managuan house where he had been killed because it was feared a bomb might be attached to it. (18)

The full story was on the front page of *La Prensa* on 10th March, which hailed the event as 'a tremendous military operation'. It turned out that the neighbours had believed the house to be empty and the driver had slept outside all night in the general's car.

The reaction to this operation was, of course, excitement on all sides. *El Perro*, deputy commander of the National Guard, was renowned as a rapist and torturer and was a focus of hatred for the whole population. The people were delighted to hear about his execution.

Sofía Montenegro later described Nora's escape as 'that spectacular flight from the biggest hunt ever mounted against a revolutionary commando.' The family home in Jinotepe was thoroughly searched by the National Guard. Nora's father Segundo was at the Chontales farm and Doña Muriel was in Caracas, where one of her relatives had died. A green Fiat 125, registered to Doña Muriel, was being sought. An order was put out by the Jinotepe National Guard to capture Nora's sister, Lidia Ruby, and detain her two brothers for questioning. Lidia was studying at the UCA and she was reported to have been with her classmates on the night of the operation. Nora's lodger, María Elena, was interrogated continuously by the Guard for several days until her mother asked for the intervention of the Permanent Commission for Human Rights. María Elena had moved out of the Altamira house for a few days, after a phone call from Nora that the house was going to be fumigated. (19)

There was much excitement on the 16th March when *La Prensa* printed a letter signed by Nora along with a photograph which had been delivered to them 'in a sealed envelope.' It was that photo which travelled around the world showing Nora, the incarnation of the future, living hope, dressed in olive green army fatigues. (20) It is believed that this powerful image inspired thousands of young people to participate in the insurrection less than a year later. 'Who can forget the sweet euphoria we all shared when we saw her dressed in army camouflage, the red and black scarf round her neck and the rifle on her shoulder in the foreground?' asked Sofía Montenegro. (21)

In the letter Nora took responsibility for the operation. In what has been described as a brazen message she said, 'I want it to be known that I participated in the operation of bringing to justice the bloody henchman.... none of my family members, friends or business associates had any involvement in the planning or implementation.'(22) But the police still believed that it was Nora and Lidia who had carried out the assassination between them.

Sister Rina Molina, a former pupil who had come back to teach at the Colegio Teresiano, said 'I couldn't believe it. When I read the official newspapers, my initial reaction was that it must be some kind of propaganda stunt. We had heard rumours that Nora was involved with the FSLN but it we didn't know until then that it was true..'

It was a shock for many people, including Nora's parents: 'Their initial response was practically to disown me.' The rôle of the temptress Eve, the suggestion that Nora might have had a sexual relationship with the General, the aspect of conspiracy, of betrayal, as well as the actual execution and Nora's flight from home, were all factors which weighed against her.

It is this action that Nora is most (in)famous for, despite her much greater later achievements. *Time* refers to Nora as 'the Mata Hari of the

Sandinista revolution.' (25) Particularly in the United States this was the image portrayed of Nora until, not long before her death, she managed to subvert it. On her death the obituary in *The Times* devoted 14 out of 21 lines to this single event. (25)

Nora claimed she felt no guilt over *El Perro's* death - firstly because the original plan was to kidnap him, secondly because she wasn't present at the execution and thirdly because, after all, 'he represented repression, he really was a monster.'

While there may always be some doubt over the operation, this manner of assassination was not within the normal pattern of FSLN action. They generally preferred to take hostages, through whom they could negotiate a series of concessions. The involvement of the FSLN in armed combat normally took the form of a guerrilla commando against National Guard squadrons. I also believe that, even if the intention was to kill him, Nora was not made party to that decision. Nora's mother still maintains that, 'The FSLN took advantage of her in that operation.'

However, despite the fact that the operation had technically failed, Nora became a national heroine. While a kidnapping would have enabled the FSLN to free political prisoners, the execution was good for popular morale and it was a massive blow to the dictator, who had lost his right hand man.

Into the Mountains

Although Nora posed confidently enough for the camera, this was not an easy time for her. The comrades managed to get her up to the Northern Front, where she undertook military training for the first time. She remembered, 'I was terrified of anything military. Because of my father I recoiled from it and I was frightened of guns.'

And of course she missed her daughters terribly. 'Through various contacts I was able to find out how my children were doing and that they were well,' she told Margaret Randall. After a short time with Nora's cousin, the girls went to live with their grandmother, Doña Muriel, who took them away to the United States for about six months, to make sure they were safe. Nora was not able to communicate with her family and they knew nothing about her.

After training, the comrades got her out of the country. She spent some time in Costa Rica where she met up with people working in exile to support the revolution, people like Dr Carlos Tünnermann from León. The Group of Twelve were also in San José at that time and this was where Nora first met Father Miguel d'Escoto, shortly before the Twelve returned to Nicaragua.

Then in June 1978, Nora was sent across the border to join the guerrilla front 'Benjamin Zeledón', (1) where she had to learn to fight, to kill and to watch her comrades die: another radical change...

Looking back on her decision to take part in operation *El Perro*, Nora said: 'It was no more than a consequence of the personal decisions I had already made and that I went on making, little by little. It's the little decisions you go on making each day that make you consistent with what you believe. This means the big decisions take you a very long time but when you make them, there's an enormous leap and you begin a new stage in your life....'

The mountains on the Southern Front are not so high, rising up to one thousand metres at their highest, on the strip of land - about twenty kilometres wide - between the great lake of Nicaragua, Lago Cocibolca, and the Pacific Ocean. From the border crossing at Peñas Blancas, running up towards Rivas, the range becomes thinner and thinner until it peters out. Down there on the plain, beside the lake, runs the Pan American Highway towards Costa Rica, through the flat bright heat of the day, with no cover, no vegetation.

At the southern end of the great lake, is another strip of land separating Nicaragua from Costa Rica. Here, small settlements like Cardenas, strung out like beads on the southern bank, sit exposed to the sun, gazing at the mud flats and, beyond, the endless shimmering water of the lake and, behind, five bare kilometres to the border.

At the south-east corner of the lake is the town of San Carlos, situated on the San Juan river. It was to this corner that the militants from the Solentiname archipelago would sail, either to take part in raids, to join the Front or to flee the country. The river practically forms the rest of the border with Costa Rica between San Carlos and San Juan del Norte on the Caribbean Coast, although for the first half there is still a distance of five or ten kilometres to cross before reaching the safety of Costa Rica. 'The broad and beautiful river in the grey dawn of the balmy summer morning', as Mark Twain described it, runs through the exuberant prehistoric tropical forest of Nueva Guinea, past the ruined castle where long ago Nelson surrendered to the Spanish. So says the Nicaraguan Tourist Board guide. But hiding out in the surrounding terrain means sleeping on swampy ground, mosquitoes, snakes.

This was the setting for the Southern Front. Primarily, the action was centred along the Pacific side, in the attempt to take Rivas, the main town of the region, about forty miles from the border, where the Insurrectionists hoped to set up their provisional government. Somoza increasingly concentrated the best of his soldiers and equipment at Peñas Blancas in order to defend this entry point. It wasn't difficult for the Guard, with

74

helicopter sweeps, to pick off the guerrilla forces in the largely uncovered terrain.

The leader of the Southern Front was Humberto Ortega. Germán Pomares (The Tapir) was one of the chiefs of staff. They built up a good base of support among the local people, establishing safe houses where they could hide the arms they had acquired until they were needed for combat. It was possible to cross the border to get further help from collaborators who might, for example, lend a car for a particular mission. Many of the collaborators in villages and farms were women though often only the men were counted.

Although there may not have been many *guerrilleros* in the mountains, there were a fair number of foreign journalists and photographers in Nicaragua who were regularly invited to visit the camps and see what was happening. Their presence not only ensured a valuable record of those times but also helped the FSLN propaganda machine. Omar Cabezas emphasised the importance of maintaining the visibility of the guerrilla in the highlands. 'The myth that the guerrilla existed in the mountain was the spark that ignited the whole country. The mountain was a political factor, not a military one. In fact the bulk of the struggle was in the cities, factory workers, farm workers, students and housewives.'(2)

When a woman's cover was blown, instead of allowing her to stay in the country, she was usually sent into exile. In contrast, the men went underground or joined the guerrilla, that highly romanticised aspect of the revolutionary struggle. Here the lines of the young poet Felipe Peña, who served on the Southern Front at the same time as Nora, convey some of the beauty of life in the mountains:

> It is half past 5 in the afternoon, the weather is calm
> and we do not hear the sound of the little plane
> > surveying the frontier
> only the mumble mumble of the comrades

chatting in their tents
and evening birdsong in the mountain
the *gongolona*, the squawker crow
 the partridge that whistles like someone lost in the wood
the *choschós*
the congo monkeys who cry *cong cong cong*
the woodpecker pecking at a dry tree
and monkeys playing among the leafy branches
shrieking and throwing down dead twigs.
This afternoon more than ever
        the crickets have been lively
singing *ree ree ree* as if announcing rain
        beginning to fall
the mountain has grown dark
        we are going to stand guard
and the others to sleep without any supper. (3)

Guerrilla life was not easy. Ana Julia Guido, who was trained by Tomás Borge and who fought in the mountains for two-and-a half years explained, 'Probably the hardest thing was building up your physical resistance. It takes about six months before you get used to the rains, the hunger and the long hikes. The hikes were the hardest part - going days and days with only a little food. And the food didn't fill or nourish you. usually it was pure carbohydrates (probably *tortilla*, the thick flat round cold unleavened cornbread of the countryside). And then there was monkey meat, which *is* nourishing...'(4)

One of Nora's teachers commented on the idea of her former pupil in the mountains, 'I just couldn't imagine Nora as a *guerrillera*. She was so refined.' As Nora herself confided in Karen De Young, a reporter from *The Washington Post*, 'Look, I'm a person who likes to drive her car to the office!' (5) In fact, early photographs of Nora as guerrilla do seem to

76

capture a certain element of surprise or discomfort on her part. She stands erect with a military bearing, rifle across her shoulder, but those sleepy eyes are cast down and away from the camera - as if she is a little shy, uncertain of the new rôle she has suddenly walked into. Possibly it is just irritation at being photographed! (6)

Other photographs show her laughing. Despite the difficulties Nora found this experience particularly enriching because of the way in which it brought her closer to her companions, her comrades. 'It was extraordinary to see how the individual experiences fused and the differences just disappeared. Share with someone the lack of food, the rain, danger, the possibility of death, and a very strong group feeling grows, a feeling of human solidarity that I have felt at no other time of my life,' she remembered in 1986.

The sense of wholeness that Nora experienced here must have come from the fact that the reality she was now living was the one she believed in; finally there was a direct relationship between thought and action. She no longer had to conspire, to dissemble, to act as an accomplice. Moreover, this new reality was one she shared with others, not a different reality because of accidents of birth, class, education, wealth.

There is a saying in Nicaragua: *la montaña educa* - the mountain teaches. Nora's position was that of a political co-ordinator, which involved leading discussions after the day's military exercises. These political study circles were part of military training and also formed part of military life. Before an operation, it was customary to sit down and review the political reasons behind the action (7).

According to Chester, most of the combatants were very young, they had not had any military preparation, they didn't really know what they were doing there. Nora, on the other hand was very clear about what she was doing. Yet Nora remembers it differently: 'I was more of a student than a teacher and those who taught me most were the *campesinos*. What I knew in theory, they were living. Basically we talked about the realities of Nicaraguan life, the conditions in our country and the Sandinista platform

77

for struggle. We had a lot of information about what was happening in other parts of Nicaragua: we were both informing and forming ourselves. We talked a lot about the objectives of our struggle - education, the position of women, health, the Atlantic Coast, fundamental rights... Everything we wanted for the future.'

While she herself claims not to have had any great political preparation, the decision to allot Nora this rôle was probably based on her interpersonal skills and her commitment in addition to her new stature in the organisation as an heroic inspiration to the young.

The peasants they got to know were not passive or negative. Omar Cabezas recalls talking to a *campesino*: 'a whole lot of memories, of ideas he had, of dreams, of whatever, of doubts, the desire to know, to ask questions.' (8) Nora was also impressed. The *campesinos* spoke with such clarity, such assurance, in a public forum, something she had always found very difficult to do.

The time that Nora spent in the mountains was important for her on a personal, as well as political, level. About a month after leaving Managua, she met up again with Chester. 'There was a meeting in a safe house and when I walked in, she was there, she jumped up and cried out 'What a wonderful surprise!' and she kissed me full on the mouth. And that's how it happened, that's how we began (as lovers)...' As Nora put it delicately, 'Despite the limitations of underground life, we had the opportunity of getting to know each other better.'

In the same interview Nora told Margaret Randall in 1980: 'We haven't had much time together, but what we've shared has been profound. When we were together in the mountains, we became very close. In that kind of struggle time takes on new dimensions. When people are able to be together in conditions like that, they tend to live with an intensity that's unusual in more normal times.'

There must have been additional reasons for this intensity. While Nora had discovered a new reality in the mountains, she had left another behind her - her daughters and her home, the intimacy of family. In order to fully live in the present, she had to deny that past reality. This denial was a shared experience among many in the guerrilla. Omar Cabezas remembers passing through León, passing his parents' home (which of course he was not allowed to visit). 'In the present, that couldn't be my house... since now I was coming from somewhere else, from living a different life... the past and the present couldn't exist together.' (9)

Nora had also suffered the painful breakdown of her marriage and endured a drawn-out sexual struggle with *El Perro*. Now she was experiencing the physical hardship of guerrilla life. She needed something! But perhaps more than anything, Nora seemed to feel she had found the true equal partnership she had been searching for, where personal and political commitment coincided. 'We fought together,' she related simply in 1980. 'My relationship with this man has been very good. As far as I'm concerned, he's close to perfect. He's an excellent comrade, very honest and understanding - a real revolutionary.'

The next time Chester met up with Nora was when he became a squadron leader with the Southern Front. The Guard had been watching him in Managua and Humberto Ortega decided to get him out of there. There was an operation planned to take the border crossing of Peñas Blancas. Chester was to lead one of the two groups.

'I knew Nora was a member of my group. I arrived at the camp to give the people instructions and I found out she was already pregnant!'

This may well have been an accident, but it was still an affirmation of life. Attitudes towards bearing children have to be seen in the context of the United States birth control programmes introduced in Nicaragua during the 60s and taken over by Somoza in the 70s: these aimed to 'kill the guerrilla in the womb' by means of enforced contraception and sterilisation in areas where the Sandinistas were known to be strongest. United States volunteers put agents into anti-polio vaccines to sterilise women without their knowledge or consent. Family planning was associated in the public mind with imperialism and AMPRONAC itself had called for the elimination of birth control. (11)

In the mountains what Nora had to come to terms with was the use of arms. This was another area where she came to surprise herself. Although she had realised the necessity of armed struggle, it was another step to actually use a weapon herself. She had not had any kind of military training for Operation *El Perro*. Her revolutionary commitment was overlaid by memories of her father, his gun, his participation in events she did not want think about: how many people had he killed?

'The idea simply terrified me,' she said. 'And when I arrived in the camp, I said to the comrades, Look, I'll do anything, but don't ask me to pick up a rifle because I just can't.' However, she had no choice. 'I remember when I held a pistol in my hands for the first time, I thought: And what do I do with this?' It was the same when she had to take her first shot. What do I do? But she persevered, taking part in the regular military training and then went into combat.

'You're always afraid in the first battle,' said another *guerrillera*, Ana Julia. 'I had never even heard gunfire before.' (usually in training, they would aim, not fire, because of the need to preserve ammunition and also because of the possibility the shots would be heard.). 'When it begins you feel a kind of desperation, but then you calm down and begin to identify the shots. By the next battle it all seems normal..' (12)

Chester was there to support Nora in her first battle. 'After the first battle you begin to have a very special relationship with your weapon,' she said, 'because your life, and the lives of your *compañeros*, depends on it. And at that time, the life of Nicaragua also depended on it.'

Nora first participated in combat as part of the medical squad: ironical to think that, ten years before, she had left medical school because she couldn't stand the sight of pain - though presumably something of what she learned in Washington came in useful. 'She used to make medical diagnoses,' recalls Chester, 'I used to say she was more like a

80

witchdoctor than anything.' 'She was *supermachista*, She had complete control over her nerves by then. If the Guard had captured and tortured her, you knew they would have got nothing out of her at all. I remember there was one of the comrades had got a leg wound. In fact she had to cut his leg off at the thigh. We knew we had nothing to close the artery with, no clip, to stop the bleeding, so we knew he was going to die. I felt awful! But when you looked at Nora's face, there was nothing that gave her away, she was completely calm.' Nora later explained, 'You rid yourself of your fears, step by step.'

Then she was a member of the mortar squad, lifting the heavy equipment and running forward, stopping and loading up, trying to keep the firing going, to provide close support for the comrades out in front. Finally she fought as a simple combatant, which is probably the most dangerous, and came to lead four squads.

According to Flor in Gioconda Belli's novel *La Mujer Habitada*, 'Each step brings its own dose of fear that you have to overcome... and at each step, as you get more responsibility, you have less opportunity to share your fear... (Additionally) for a woman, when we're faced with new tasks, we have to face an internal struggle - a struggle to convince ourselves inside that we can do it.'

'Each time I go into battle,' Nora said, 'I have to conquer my fear. In battle I felt cold, without feeling. That is a defence mechanism, especially if you are a sensitive person.' (13) Despite all these problems, Nora admitted that she grew to like military life 'I saw comrades die, of course. The nearness of death teaches you a great deal. '

The fact that Nora was pregnant with her third baby lent an added significance to her participation in armed combat: shooting at - and killing - the National Guard, she was fighting for the life of her child, for all the children.

A woman's life in the guerrilla forces had certain liberating aspects. 'In most cases you weren't even thought of as a woman or a man - you were

81

simply one comrade among many. Most of us, particularly the women, had never had that experience before. I think women were accepted and appreciated as comrades by everyone. In training the same was expected from us as from men.' And so it was in combat.

However, in other ways, the *guerrilleras* had support from their male comrades. 'In normal everyday tasks - hauling water, for example - the men always helped.' (14)

In the regulations of the organisation, intimate relations between comrades were not approved of, although they certainly did occur. It is not easy to say how common a relationship such as Nora's would have been in the mountains, where opportunities for intimacy were severely limited. Usually the guerrilla slept in their clothes, although 'sometimes they were allowed to take off their boots,' notes Gioconda Belli in her novel. Omar Cabezas recommended that men not think about women at all while they were in the mountains, 'so as not to martyr yourself.' (15)

Tomás Borge described the conditions: 'You sleep alone, accompanied by the cold, by dreams of bonfires and bakeries and burning sand, your only thought that early in the morning, before sunrise, you have to get up. And that weighs more than a ton: you have to get out of your warm clothes and put on your damp ones. If you don't, the next night you'll have two sets of wet clothing and feel as though a dog had run his moist nose all over your body.' (16)

It has also been suggested that most men would actually prefer, for a lover, 'the woman at home' rather than the 'comrade' who fought alongside them. Omar Cabezas talks about his girlfriend Claudia: 'she was the flag I carried in my hand into the mountain, so that I wouldn't get wet or muddy... I slept with my flag, I folded it up neatly and put it under my head...' (17)

Nora's own experience of being a woman in the mountain was probably mediated by her status in the organisation, her main rôle as political co-ordinator rather than military leader, her relationship with Chester and, also, the fact that she was pregnant. She remembered how all the comrades took care of her without paternalism. 'They'd look for guavas and if they found fruit they'd give it to me.' And she told Margaret Randall, 'The comrades were always trying to help me so that I wouldn't have to lift heavy weights.' Additionally, Nora carried with her a social ease and confidence that enabled her to make her own space in whatever circumstances.

Towards the end of August 1978, there was great excitement about the news of the assault on the National Palace. A commando unit, led by Eden Pastora and Dora María Téllez (warname Patricia), had taken over the Palace while Congress was in session. They were disguised in National Guard uniforms. Somoza had to pay half a million dollars in ransom, and even his own newspaper published the Sandinista communiqué. He was also forced to free a whole busload of political prisoners including Tomás Borge. Crowds of people came out to line the streets, to cheer them all as the bus drove to the airport from where they were flown out to Panama. The dictator was completely humiliated by this action. (18)

Tomás Borge was finally free after two and a half years, keeping up resistance in a variety of ways: hunger strikes, writing, and political discussion. Doris Tijerino (Conchita) who had been recaptured in April, was also released.

The National Palace raid stimulated uprisings in Matagalpa, then in September, under FSLN leadership, in Estelí, Masaya and León. Women in AMPRONAC had become increasingly involved in political action. On Mothers' Day earlier that year they had demonstrated under the slogan 'The Best Gift Would Be A Free Nicaragua.' Those members who argued that it was possible to reform the government rather than fight for a total transformation of society increasingly found themselves in a minority. After a national ballot in July the Association declared itself Sandinista. In August, when the government raised the price of staple goods, women - armed with empty pots and pans - marched through the streets of Managua and other cities to protest at the economic policies. In local communities women performed in street theatre, with skits entitled 'Our Children are Hungry.'

Repressive measures in retaliation against the insurrection drew on all Somoza's military power - bombings, search and destroy missions and random invasions of neighbourhoods. (19)

Nora's chief of staff while she was in the mountains was 'Martin', a guerrilla priest whose real name was Gaspar García Laviana. Coming from Spain and having worked as a missionary of the Sacred Heart for nine years, he gave up his parish in Tola, a small town in the Rivas province, on Christmas Day 1977 and sent an open letter to the Nicaraguan people. 'It is time to close ranks around the Sandinista Front, to join our hands and our arms, because the sound of the guns of justice in our mountains, towns and villages, is the sign of redemption drawing near... The Somoza system is a sin and to free ourselves from oppression is to free us from sin... With my gun in my hand, full of faith and love for my Nicaraguan people, I will fight to my last breath for the coming of the kingdom of justice in our homeland.' (20)

From all accounts, Martin had a great deal of presence. In appearance, dressed in olive green, with the beret and heavy army boots, hair curling onto his collar and the Che Guevara moustache, a rifle over his shoulder, he was the archetypal *guerrillero*. He was calm, but very dynamic and hardworking. And he had a great capacity for enjoying life. This was the comrade that Nora shared a shack with on the Southern Front. 'He was my companion, my friend; I'll never forget my relationship with him.' And Gioconda Belli's novel emphasises how living and fighting together 'you get to know each other very well, you lower your defences, you talk of your dreams and doubts...'

Martin took great care of Nora because of the baby she was carrying. Perhaps, although she had become separated from the Church and Gaspar himself had left his calling, Nora looked towards him as a means of spiritual connection for her unborn child. And it is likely that they discussed aspects of the Church, liberation theology, the apparent contradiction in a priest taking part in armed struggle...

There was certainly a special bond between them. 'He said to me once: "It may be that I won't still be here when I triumph. But if you cry when I die, it will trouble me greatly. The most I will allow you is that someday you will bring me a bunch of small flowers, but they must be from the countryside. And no-one must go around crying because I will always be deeply involved in the struggle."'

Maybe Martin had a presentiment of his own death. In December 1978, he was assigned to the war front which was established all along the Costa Rican border. He and Alejandro Guevara were sent with a small squadron to take over a *hacienda*. 'The area was practically impassable, just mud and puddles. That was a night of terrible rain, we arrived at three in the morning, trembling with cold, at the side of a roaring river.' (21) The Guard had found out they were to be at the farm and started firing on sight. 'They were about 40 and we were ten. They surrounded us. Gaspar was one of the first to fall. At the end there were only three of us still facing them while the others retreated down the river.' (22)

Regardless of the request he had made earlier, Nora was unable to come to terms with Martin's death. 'It affected me so deeply that I couldn't cry. When they told me, I didn't react. Everyone who knew the enormous affection I had for him asked me why I didn't cry.' This was a problem that affected so many in the struggle.

Flor, in *La Mujer Habitada* , tells Lavinia: 'That's happened to me recently. I can't believe in the death of my comrades. I don't react. I don't know if one of these days I'm going to start crying and never be able to stop... We simply reject it. We carry on believing we'll see those comrades alive... we'll meet them all at the triumph.' Often 'there was no time, there was no space for crying.' Many experienced psychological problems later because of this lack of opportunity to grieve.

Not long after Martin's death, when she was around six or seven months pregnant, Nora was told she had to leave the guerrilla camp and go back to the city. 'I didn't want to. I thought I was still in shape to be in the mountains.' (23)

Chester reveals that, 'It was really difficult for me, she was there with her great belly, and there was nothing to eat, just rice and the guava tree, she ate nothing but guavas. But I couldn't, I wouldn't, impose anything on her personally. I had a great respect for her, not just because I loved her. She had made up her mind she wanted to stay...' To get round Nora's strong will, Chester asked the leaders for help. 'I insisted they take her out.'

Humberto Ortega told her, 'You can't let your personal feelings get in the way. You are too far along for us to feel comfortable about your being here.' Nora related, 'So they sent me to the city... They took me out of there.' There is an element of defiance in the way she puts this: she makes it clear this was not a decision that she agreed with, it was an order - but Nora always followed orders. It was part of the FSLN statutes 'to immediately obey orders without question or hesitation' (24)

In fact Nora was sent down to San José, where she carried out various tasks in support of the movement. She was in charge of finances for the Southern Front, which was logical, given her knowledge of the situation there, and of supplies in general. But she was also involved in propaganda work, as were many women militants at that time.

Her son, Alberto Segundo (named after her father), was born in San José in April 1979. Nora also took the opportunity of sending for her two daughters, now that she was in a place of safety. 'She contacted me from Costa Rica,' says Doña Muriel. 'I didn't know anything about her... everyone said she was dead... or they said they'd seen her somewhere else... She told me she was about to have another baby and I went over there, to spend a few days with her.'

Doña Muriel provided Nora with support at this time even though she was still hurt about her daughter's involvement in the *El Perro* operation. This was never resolved openly between them. 'Of course, with the new baby, there was no time then to talk about what she'd done,' recalls Doña Muriel.

Chester also managed to get to San José for Alberto's birth. It seems that it was from him that Muriel got most of her information about the military operation, about his relationship with Nora, about life in the mountains and Nora's friendship with Gaspar. Chester's impression of Doña Muriel was of a strong, brave woman, with a good sense of humour - a description which could be applied to Nora herself. Chester and Doña Muriel always maintained good relations with each other, despite the changing circumstances.

The baby was born as many of Nora's friends died. Around the same time, some of the *guerrilleros* from her old squadron joined the Nueva Guinea Front, which was an attempt to move into the centre of Nicaragua from the South-East. The 126-strong column succeeded in diverting massive Somoza forces to the region, but they were surprised and almost the whole column was wiped out. Nora was overcome by grief at the news and wept for all the young comrades she had fought with in the Southern Front.

By the time the triumph came, Tomás Borge was the only one of the original founders of the FSLN to be left alive. Despite the sadness at the deaths of her comrades, Nora said, 'After the triumph I would have been happy to stay in the army... With a little training, I'd be quite willing to return to combat, if the gringos come...' However, the FSLN had other tasks for her to fulfil, other *trincheras* - trenches on a different battlefield.

The Triumph

In Costa Rica, though still dressed in olive green and officially still a member of the army, Nora returned to something of the comforts of her old life. She lived in a villa with hot and cold running water, clean white sheets and a cool shady courtyard with bright flowers where she could sit after work. There was no need to speak in whispers, cautious of the carrying wind.

Despite the persistence of the United States in supporting Somoza, Costa Rica - along with Panama, Mexico and Venezuela in the region and several Western European social democrat parties - now openly demonstrated their support for the FSLN. And San José, only a stone's throw away from the border with Nicaragua and the Southern Front, was home to a great many Nicaraguans working in one way or other for the revolution.

In Costa Rica Nora came into contact with other women involved in propaganda work. Rosario Murillo had been in charge of the Sandinista foreign information service in Costa Rica for well over a year. She was a couple of years younger than Nora, but had also been at the Colegio Teresiano for a while before going off to finishing schools in England and Switzerland. She was a great-niece of Sandino himself and had worked at the opposition paper *La Prensa* from the early 1970s as Pedro Joaquim Chamorro's personal assistant, and got to know Daniel Ortega closely in Costa Rica.

Michèle Najlis had been in Costa Rica with her baby son since the earthquake in 1972, first as a member of the Costa Rican Communist Party and then later involved in solidarity tasks.

Gioconda Belli had been in Costa Rica since 1976. She worked in the FSLN foreign relations commission and travelled widely to represent the revolutionary struggle: 'Gioconda speaks in Paris' is how she wryly refers to her work in this period. 'I always had this sense that I was treated

differently because I was a woman. But let the men have the glory, I said.'
(1)

Another was Dora María Téllez (Patricia) who had commanded the assault on the National Palace. She had acted as spokesperson for the commando in Panama City where 'journalists from every major news service clamoured for the story of how the young revolutionaries had brought the dictator to his knees.' (2) She had contact with solidarity committees, the Panamanian authorities and was involved in obtaining material aid.

The birth of Nora's third child can be seen in the context of the great belief in the future that she shared with the other women working for the revolutionary cause. Dora María, for example, wrote after the first delivery she took charge of as a medical student: 'Have I completed my mission by delivering this child? No, our work will only be done when we can give these new ones a new world, a different world... and I must be committed to the birth of that new world.' (3)

The writing was on the wall now for Somoza. In October 1978 the United States mediation team, although they wanted to secure Somoza's resignation, had rejected the proposal of the Broad Opposition Front (FAO) that the FAO form a government. The Group of Twelve soon withdrew from the talks, claiming that the United States plan would merely mean *Somocismo* without Somoza. In February 1979, the FSLN established the National Patriotic Front, comprising the United Popular Movement, the unions, the Group of Twelve, the Independent Liberals and the Social Christian Party in a common front against the dictatorship. In March the three FSLN tendencies were officially reunified.

However, the United States continued to finance the Somoza régime: nearly $200 million in 1978 and another $95 million in 1979, as US fears of a new FSLN offensive grew. Somoza received military aid from Guatemala and El Salvador along with important supplies of arms from Israel - who also sent a team of military experts to Nicaragua to install an air defence system. United States military aircraft from the Panama Canal Zone were flying in weapons for the National Guard, although officially military assistance had been cut off in September 1978. (4)

The Final Offensive was launched by the united FSLN at the end of May 1979. Five different Fronts attacked key Somoza strongholds in unison and broadcast from within Nicaragua itself, calling for insurrection and a general strike: 'Heroic people of Nicaragua, the hour of the overthrow of the infamous dictator is come...' (5)

Radio Sandino was the clandestine radio station, the voice of freedom for Nicaragua, the official voice of the Sandinista Front during the last months of the insurrection. Nora's old friend Daisy Zamora was responsible for programming. 'The warrior's drumbeat', as the station was nicknamed, promised to 'continue to bring you information until the last notes, the last voices, until the last skirmishes are over, until dawn breaks over the whole of Nicaragua.' *Radio Sandino* brought news of the success of the fronts, the loss of comrades: 'At 10.30 the general barracks of the Somocista Guard was taken in the city of León... Long live the heroic women ... Long live the fallen heroes and martyrs of León... let's follow their example... everybody to the people's insurrection... Somoza is going, the people remain... victory is ours.' (6)

On June 2nd the FSLN entered León, led by, among others, Dora María Téllez with Leticia Herrera. Two days later the general strike began - with massive response - and the FSLN took León, the first city to be wholly liberated from the Guard. Dora María said later that the overwhelming female presence in the high command in León was pure coincidence - or rather, a consequence of the massacre at Veracruz in April which wiped out several leading Sandinistas. But she emphasised that what wasn't a coincidence was her designation as head of command. (7)

Things were moving so quickly. Even at a distance (from Costa Rica) it seemed difficult to catch your breath. When Somoza saw for definite that he was losing, he ordered the indiscriminate bombing of towns, factories, churches, hospitals. There was insurrection in Managua.

90

Women were closely involved in the final struggle for freedom. Since the strikes of the previous August, the women's movement, AMPRONAC, had been forced underground, drawing on its national structure to create a large clandestine organising force. It set up safe houses, lines of communication between popular organisations and the FSLN, and secret hospitals. Women began to organise civil defence committees against incursions by the Guard in their neighbourhoods. In Estelí and Monimbó, where fighting was amongst the heaviest in the country, women set up an intelligence system to alert their neighbours to the presence of the National Guard by switching lights on and off and banging pots and pans. (8)

Daisy Zamora remembered, 'the Civil Defence Committees building barricades, all the *barrios* of Managua lit up with bonfires... I don't recognise this lost city of mine... destroyed by earthquake, razed by dictatorship... scorched by the implacable sun.' (9)

Amada Pineda, a country woman who was tortured so severely by the Guard that she had to go to the USSR to receive medical treatment, recounts her activities on her return to Managua. 'We fought with whatever we had. We took everything they fired at us and sent it right back to them: mortars and even bombs when they fell from the planes and didn't explode. We'd look for them, disarm them, fill them with fresh explosives and send them back. One day we found a 500 pound bomb. We had a hard time digging it out because it made such a deep hole, but we managed . We split it in half. One half was placed on the Bello Horizonte bridge, the other we sent somewhere else. When the FSLN retreated to Masaya, we went with them. Later they told us the Guard was scared to go into the house where we'd been because they were afraid it was mined and would blow up. They discovered we weren't just a bunch of two-bit kids fighting with molotov cocktails or with machetes ... Most of us in that house were women, but we fought with everything we had.' (10)

91

President Carter tried to persuade the Organisation of American States to agree to send in 'a peace-keeping force' (which would have been in fact a military intervention to prevent a FSLN victory) but the OAS, for the first time ever, defied the United States. Unilateral intervention by the United States was virtually impossible - especially after the film of an ABC correspondent being shot down in cold blood by Somoza's National Guard was shown on US television.(11)

Back in Costa Rica, the provisional Junta of National Reconstruction was set up, representing a range of political interests. The five-person junta consisted of Daniel Ortega, Sergio Ramírez, Violeta Chamorro, Alfonso Robelo, and Moisés Hassan.

The United States intensified its efforts to influence the provisional government and to ensure that the National Guard remain intact, thus prolonging the war. They nominated five other members to be included in the government, including Ernesto Fernandez, the financial secretary of Somoza's Liberal Party and a close confidante of the dictator. Costa Rica and Venezuela supported this attempt to introduce more 'moderate' elements into the new government.(12)

On 24th June the FSLN took the Guard barracks in Masaya and the Somoza forces abandoned the city. They took refuge in their headquarters where they remained under siege. Dora María Téllez was one of the commanders who divided the city into military zones to organise the support from the *barrios*. The whole zone from Masaya to Granada was taken.

Fearing drastic reprisals, the FSLN ordered a strategic retreat from Managua to Masaya. Six thousand people left Managua secretly at night, walking the twenty-eight kilometres, carrying their babies and some of their belongings out of danger. After the triumph, this retreat was celebrated annually on June 27th by large numbers of people making the same night time march. Tyres were burnt alongside the path to symbolise the aerial bombings ...

In the morning the Guard found the capital almost deserted. The dictator could only stay in power by killing every Nicaraguan. The Guard began killing any youngsters over thirteen in the streets, regardless of whether they were FSLN supporters or not. (13)

Ernesto Cardenal visited Daisy at the radio station to tape his prophecy for the ordinary soldiers of the National Guard - there wouldn't be room for them in Somoza's private plane when the dictator fled the country. (14)

The FSLN took Matagalpa. Then they took the Guard barracks in Estelí.

On July 17th the news came through to headquarters in San José: 'We have won the war. The dictatorship is liquidated.' (15) Somoza had resigned. He'd packed his bags and flown to Miami. The older officers of the National Guard were to leave the country. Without leadership the National Guard collapsed.

The Junta flew back to Nicaragua and a new government was installed at León University the next day.

The FSLN entered Managua in trucks and jeeps on July 19th 1979 when all the Fronts converged on the capital. They say there were a quarter of a million people there to welcome them, many sitting up on the ruins of the old cathedral, hanging from the windows. The Junta and the FSLN leadership arrived from León the following day to find the huge crowds still celebrating the Triumph.

Omar Cabezas recalled, 'I had dreamed about the Triumph but I didn't really know what it would be like. When we drove into the *Plaza de la Revolución* it was a scene of incredible happiness, of psychic and physical pleasure. A sea of people, laughter streaming off their bodies, happiness pouring from their hair. It was a dream come true.'(16) Tomás Borge walked through the crowds and women fought their way forward to kiss and embrace him. Daniel Ortega spoke from the middle of the crowd through a microphone, 'The people have overcome.'

Gioconda Belli, in the back of one of the trucks, passing through the streets surrounded by 'the beautiful faces of my people' wanted ' to grow lots of arms so that I could embrace all of them and tell them I love them.' But her joy 'hurt like childbirth' because she remembered all those comrades who had died for this dream, because she wasn't able to wake them to 'see this crowd of people coming out of the night... in this drunkenness of freedom that invades the streets and makes the trees sway.' (17)

For Nora, as for many others, it was a great disappointment not to be there. 'I thought about it,' says Chester, 'but it just wasn't possible.'

Doris Tijerino said: 'For someone like myself who had been involved in the struggle continuously since 1965, that was a time I should have been able to spend here, on the inside. But it wasn't to be. The leadership wanted me on the outside, working in the area of solidarity, so that's where I remained. And it was tremendously frustrating for me. In fact, I wasn't even here on July 19th... I wasn't able to savour the sweet taste of triumph.' (18)

Nora flew straight back to Managua. When she drove from the airport towards home, she saw the mess that had been left behind. The barricades were still up - Somoza's infamous paving stones had been ripped up to make them. There were bombed out houses with nothing left but rubble and ashes, edifices pockmarked with machine gun bullets, and red and black slogans splashed across the walls. There was still the smell of burning tyres.

She remembered, 'We went into the National Palace and said to each other: Well, what do we do now? We were without water, light, communications, healthcare, the whole infrastructure had been destroyed.'

The struggle for social justice cost the Nicaraguan people dearly. There were 35-40,000 dead and 100,000 wounded; 40,000 children orphaned; 200,000 families made homeless; and a total material damage to the economy of around US$1,810 million. In addition Somoza left behind a crushing national debt of US$1.5 billion. (19)

Immediately, the Civil Defence Committees were renamed the Sandinista Defence Committees and given responsibility for the distribution of basic food supplies, housing, care of orphans. Many women took on these tasks at local level.

There had been an outburst of looting and vandalism in the cities straight after the Triumph and members of the Guard had been killed without trial. Tomás Borge was made Head of Security and Minister of the Interior with Luis CarriÛn as his Deputy Minister. A Law for the Maintenance of Order and Public Security was passed.

The middle-class Sandinista women were put into official positions. Nora was Deputy Minister of Justice for a week. Then she was put in charge of finances for the newly created Sandinista army. 'We didn't have anything,' she recalled. 'They gave you a job and you had to do everything, from finding people to do the job and a house to do it in, to inventing the mechanisms. From nothing. They would say to you, you are in charge! And you had to figure out how to do it. Everything was your responsibility and you didn't have any experience. It was an extraordinary stage in the revolution. We did it from nothing!' 'We had to start from scratch and set up the system. I knew almost nothing about financial systems but I had an excellent group of comrades to work with.' (20)

Gioconda Belli was put in charge of the television system. 'I went with a group of comrades - we were all armed - and walked into Channel 6. I gathered everyone together and spoke to them. I said they could stay on if they wanted. We didn't have money to pay them right away but that we'd provide them with food.' (21)

The vacated mansions of the dictator, his family and National Guard officers were taken over as new ministries and other national services were created. The comrades worked in makeshift offices, using whatever furniture they could get hold of. All official buildings were guarded by the FSLN in olive green, with rifles slung over their shoulder.

95

Of course there were many errors due to inexperience, as Omar Cabezas recalls: 'We had very romantic ideas of reality. We made some mistakes in economic planning. For instance we sacrificed the cotton crop so that we could grow basic grains for everyone and we lost US$100 million that would have given us income, cash for machinery...' (22)

Despite such problems Nora said, 'the strongest feeling I remember from those early days is freedom. To walk freely down the streets and find a whole bunch of people I had not seen in so long. We all lived a year or more in which neither food nor sleep had any place, they just weren't necessary. We had so much inside and so much to do that the boundaries of normal life were broken. Nothing was like the past. It was a kind of dream, not because we lived outside reality, but because it felt like a dream that Somoza had been defeated. Life had different dimensions...'

Yet her homecoming was not entirely joyful. Nora had experienced many profound changes in the sixteen months that she had been away from Managua. She had lived in difficult and dangerous conditions and felt the death of many comrades. She had had to adjust to living without her daughters, to having no contact at all with them. Now she was returning home to her beloved city, her own free country, with a new baby, and thrilled to be with her family once more. What she hadn't anticipated was their response to her activities and this must have caused her a lot of private grief. Her parents were only just recovering from the unexpected blow they had received from her involvement in operation *El Perro*. 'It took a long time before they could even attempt to understand what I had done.. In time they did understand although it hasn't been easy for them,'(23) While Doña Muriel rejected what her own daughter had done, she had taken responsibility for her granddaughters. And now, there was another grandchild to take care of, as Nora threw herself into new political tasks.

Unfortunately Nora's father died in an accident not long after the Triumph. This meant that Doña Muriel soon went to live with Nora and the children. However, the changes that were taking place in the country were undermining the life she had known and the political distance between Nora and her mother was still vast.

Nora's reunion with her daughters had not been easy. While she had been away, her two daughters had lived with their grandparents. Jorgé, who had always kept in contact with them since the marriage broke up, had taken the opportunity to reclaim paternity. The girls had lived through insurrections and indiscriminate bombings. Now suddenly they were back with their mother, who had appeared in battle dress, with a baby brother they knew nothing about. The first thing little Muriel said to Nora when she saw her again was: 'One day you were at home and the next you'd gone. You never told me where. You didn't even write to me. You abandoned me.' She would often say: 'If you had just told me that you had to go away I might have understood. But what I couldn't understand was that you never told me anything.' (24)

For Muriel it was particularly hard because 'first her father went away to Mexico and then her mother went to the guerrilla.' Little Dafne had been too young to suffer this double desertion in the same way. But anyway, everyone agrees that Dafne was like her mother both in her looks and her character - she was very strong, very calm, said Nora's mother.

Nora also adopted the son of a woman friend who had died in the war. Roberto Carlo was one and a half years old when he came to live with them, Doña Muriel remembers.

It was a difficult time for all of them. Nora had to go back into her old house, where *El Perro's* assassination had taken place. It had all been such a long time ago. It was very difficult to come suddenly back into her past and try to marry the new present with other pasts that had diverged. Again she was trying to reconcile different realities - into a single reality.

When Chester came back from the mountains, there was a new son-in-law, a new father, to take into the family. Here was the man who had been part of the conspiracy in operation *El Perro* and had been responsible for taking Nora out of Managua. Like everyone who was so busy at this stage, Chester didn't spend much time at home either, nor even in Managua. He was still in the Sandinista Armed Forces, rounding up Somocista sympathisers. They might come together for brief passionate moments. Nora's relationship with him was 'almost perfect', but they never got married - maybe because they were too busy, maybe because Nora wanted to have a relationship on a different footing to the one she'd had previously.

There can be no question that it was Doña Muriel who held the family together. She provided the vital back-up that Nora needed, she kept the children happy and ran the household. This continued to be a common pattern in Nicaragua, even in families where the mother had opposing political views to their revolutionary daughters. 'My rearguard was important,' says Michèle Najlis, 'my mother and a woman called Marita, my old Nanny. I know that I've been able to work as I have, especially when my children were small, because there were two other women there to take up the slack.' (25)

The pattern of Nora's new work for Nicaragua, could surely not have been possible without the untiring support of Doña Muriel. It was a surreal life, working through the night with the comrades, chain smoking, looking up suddenly to see that dawn was breaking. Someone says, 'I'm hungry. Let's drive down to the market'. They would tumble into a jeep and drive down the road, to find the market women lighting their fires, flattening their tortillas, grumbling, 'Here come the *comandantes*. Don't you ever sleep? We're not ready yet, you'll have to wait.'

She would return home some time to pick up baby Alberto, to cradle and cosset him, hear his gurgles and have her hair pulled. She would greet her daughters - crumpled and grumbling from sleep, yet holding out their soft smooth arms for an embrace, lifting their faces for kisses - hold them close and stroke their shining hair. Then, she would have to tear herself away again, tears in her eyes. Yet she would leave with steps springing, with that feeling of power and purpose, knowing that now, after so many years of longing, she could really change things - she was involved in creating a new reality for Nicaragua.

Within fifteen days of the Triumph, the FSLN called upon AMPRONAC to contact its members and to set about building a new women's organisation alongside the other new mass organisations. This association took a new name, AMNLAE, after the first woman militant to die in combat (Nicaraguan Association of Women 'Luisa Amanda Espinosa'). Its main aim was 'to maintain the mobilisation of women around the defence and consolidation of the revolution'. (26)

The Association had success in achieving legal reform. On August 16th 1979 the Fundamental Statute of Rights and Guarantees - which declared equality for all and outlawed sex discrimination - was passed. This specifically established the right to investigate the paternity of illegitimate children, an attempt to ensure men would take paternal responsibility in a society where women were (and still are) often left holding the baby.

Since the Triumph, many of the AMPRONAC leadership, like Nora, had taken up political tasks not specifically oriented towards women's issues. Lea Guido, for example, was made the first Minister for Social Welfare. Milú Vargas was later legal counsel to the Council of State (this was the legislative body set up alongside the Junta for National Reconstruction, and comprised representatives of different political parties, trades unions and popular organisations). Here she argued that, 'laws are the weapons to fight for women's emancipation, they are never a solution to the problem.'

Other militant women were also put into high ranking positions. Daisy Zamora, for example, was made Deputy Minister of Culture, working with Ernesto Cardenal. All these women were lucky enough to be directed into posts where they could build on existing skills and interests.

Others were not so lucky. There was a great deal of misplaced talent but 'in that kind of atmosphere, in the euphoria of those first few months, who was going to feel discriminated against?' recalled Gioconda Belli in 1994.

Michèle Najlis was sent by Tomás Borge from Radio Sandino to work under him in the Ministry of the Interior and take charge of Immigration with that 'phrase you heard everywhere back then: If you can't find out how it's done, invent it.' (27)

Gioconda Belli was persuaded by her lover Henry Ruiz to leave her post of responsibility in television and work for him at the Ministry of Planning - a kind of combination secretary and bodyguard. 'That mistake cost me. I never got the same kind of respect again.' Looking back, Gioconda Belli can see the writing on the wall of a wider problem. 'As soon as victory began to seem like a possibility, things began to change, that's when we women who had been active participants in the struggle began to be forced out, to lose power, to be marginalised. In June 1979 when the tendencies were reunited and they began to organise different groups of comrades to carry out different tasks, all the leaders were men. I remember how I protested. But no one even bothered to give me an answer. I don't think women fought for power the way the men did. Maybe I was too romantic. And we paid for our romanticism.' (28)

The National Directorate of the Sandinista National Liberation Front consisted of nine men: Daniel Ortega, Humberto Ortega, Tomás Borge, Jaime Wheelock, Victor Tirado, Bayardo Arce, Luis Carrión, Henri Ruiz, and Carlos Nuñez Téllez. Dora María Téllez held the rank of *comandante* but was not a member of the Directorate. However, she was Deputy President of the Council of State from 1979 onwards and often regarded as an unofficial addition to the all-male Directorate. (29)

Nora herself was lucky enough to be moved on, after about two months, from running army finances into a job which did require her professional skills and experience. 'Responding to another directive', as she put it, she was made Special Attorney General. Her job was to bring to justice the 7,500 ex-members of the National Guard and other functionaries of the

Somoza régime who had been detained by the Sandinista army. 'It wasn't easy' was a typical understatement of Nora's to describe this new challenge.

The Tribunals

The magazine *Envio*, when reviewing the development of justice in Nicaragua, said: 'A revolution that does not treat its losers to the firing squad has a real problem on its hands.' (1) But despite the difficulties, the new government was committed to making the values of the new society work in the penitentiary and the judicial system. One problem was that, as Nora put it rather ironically in 1980, 'here in Nicaragua there never was what you might call official justice... We've had to put together a legal system from almost nothing.' (2)

At the time of the insurrection and during the following weeks, between 7000 and 8000 former members of the National Guard and civilian supporters of the previous régime were taken into custody. This was a huge number of prisoners for a country crippled by debt and war damage to maintain. By contrast, the number of people charged with espionage and treason by the French government at the end of the second World War was only 4,598.

Nora had a staff of nine, 'a fine group of people working on the project', and she showed remarkable faith in the face of the enormous task ahead of her when she told Margaret Randall in an interview at the time, 'I'm confident we'll be able to handle the job.'

Nora's team spent around a month setting up the principles and processes of revolutionary justice. This important and difficult political task was carried out in the context of the human rights record of the new régime and was thus highly visible.

On November 15th Tomás Borge admitted that many abuses of power had taken place under the new government - including torture and murder - and swore that this would stop: 'the revolution was fought to end abuses and ill-treatment... we can't abandon the basic moral principles for which so many died.' (3) In fact, out of the 419 people reported as having disappeared following detention between July and December 1979, 301 of these occurred in July when order had not been fully restored and the new government had not been able to disarm the less disciplined units which had participated in the insurrection. (4) The death penalty was officially abolished on August 23rd.

Under Nora's leadership broad rights for the accused were established; the right to silence and the right to legal counsel. Family members could not be compelled to testify. Torture was prohibited along with any kind of brutality or other intimidating interrogation tactics intended to wear the accused down - otherwise the case could be thrown out on procedural grounds. (5)

Cases were researched in detail, as Nora described. 'There was a desire to make fair decisions. We had a group of *compañeros* who would go to where the Guard member had lived to get information, to investigate why he had joined the Guard, how he had behaved, what he had done.... I'm not saying we were never unjust. It's difficult to be fair a hundred percent of the time, but we made a tremendous effort.'

On the 5th December 1979, during *Purisima* and just before Nora's 31st birthday, the Special Tribunals were set up by Decree 185. They consisted of nine special courts and three appeal courts. The tribunals were also known as the 'People's Courts' because the trials were open and ordinary people could take part - this served both to increase popular knowledge of the law and to increase its legal safeguards. The lawyer Mario Mejía was in charge of the tribunals so, although Nora was in charge of the whole operation, she did not actually take part in court. Judges were either law students or leading Sandinistas. Because of the number of cases, each trial was to take a maximum of one week. The defendants were mainly soldiers from the ranks, since their officers had either managed to escape or been allowed to leave the country just before the final triumph. (6)

A large house was taken over for the tribunals and turned into makeshift courtrooms, guarded by young soldiers in white shirts and carrying rifles. Nora had a small, almost barren office. Next door, the Special Courts office was filled with dozens of young people all involved in preparing trials for those who for so many years had abused and tortured the nation. (7)

Margaret Randall, who visited Nora to interview her, remembers her generosity of spirit and her willingness to take time out from a very busy schedule in order to tell her story. At the time she remarked, 'Nora speaks intimately about her life, but what she says relates to many women of her class and culture... Her sensitivity comes through at all times.' (8)

Margaret took a photograph of Nora on the day the first prisoner was sentenced. The Special Attorney General is standing on the landing outside one of the courts, her hair tied back in a pony tail. She is wearing a pretty smock with a bow tied at the neck, carrying a large handbag over one arm, and she is visibly pregnant (for the fourth time) and in the background stand two young soldiers holding rifles. It is a picture which reflects the many facets of the revolution.

By the beginning of 1980 the special courts were in full operation and the trials were reported daily in the newspapers. There were photographs of the war criminals and details of the 'cynical denials' of men who had obviously committed great crimes. '*Nada saben...Nada han hecho*' (They know nothing, they've done nothing) ran one headline in *Barricada* - the newspaper which had been established as the FSLN mouthpiece. (9)

Photographs of those about to go to trial were also published, with a request to members of the public to bring evidence about them to special offices around the country: '*el pueblo acusa a sus enemigos.... el pueblo hará justicia!*' (the people accuse their enemies, the people will make justice). (10)

Nora also makes a comment about the people's attitudes to justice: 'For me, one of the most interesting and wonderful things about those days was to see people who would arrive to hand over to us a Guard member and say, "Look, this is a criminal and he's out loose." And they'd hand him over to you. There was never a spirit of revenge among us... The

104

Nicaraguan people are not bitter. We're not people who hold resentments for a long time. Above all, there is love and generosity in this country.'

In his position as Minister of the Interior, Tomás Borge revenged himself on those members of the Guard who had tortured him - by forgiving them. Luis Enrique Mejía Godoy based a song on Tomás' words.

My personal revenge will be your children's
right to schooling and to flowers . . .

My personal revenge will be to greet you
'Good morning!' in streets with no beggars . . .

My personal revenge will be to give you
these hands you once ill-treated
with all their tenderness intact. (11)

Tomás said, 'We're involved in a different war now, the struggle against backwardness and ignorance, the struggle to instil in every revolutionary heart a love for the people.' (12) Thus the ethos of clemency was established at the highest level among the leadership.

Seventy prisoners had been released by the Junta on 24th December 1979 in a Christmas amnesty and a further 180 - who had fled into foreign embassies - were allowed to leave the country on 28th December. (13)

On the other hand, there is evidence that not everyone was prepared to forgive the crimes of the National Guard. 'Not even his brother wants to defend him' was a headline in *Barricada* on 12th January 1980.

It was common throughout the struggle for liberation and the whole revolutionary process after the Triumph for families to be split ideologically; when family members who were Somocista were captured and tried, this resulted in deep distress to their Sandinista siblings or children. Sofía Montenegro, for example, recounts how a year before the Triumph, her brother - an officer, a very proud member of the National

Guard - had defied her father's dying wish to leave the Guard. By their father's deathbed, he had told his siblings, 'Look kids, in this room, we're brothers and sisters. But if we come upon each other in the street and you have a gun and so do I, you'd better shoot. Because you can be sure I will.' When Sofía heard from Dora María Téllez that her brother had refused to leave Nicaragua and had been captured in León on July 18th 1979, she recalls, 'Victory turned bitter for me. Why didn't he escape? Why didn't they just kill him? He asked for a trial befitting an officer. He was one of those war machines, trained by the United States; an expert in counter-insurgency... My mother begged me to intercede on his behalf. But I had to tell her I couldn't - I would have had to intercede for all the National Guard.' (14)

There were other instances where the people were not as forgiving as Nora liked to remember. On 26th January 1980 a demonstration of mothers, who had lost children in the fighting, was organised by AMNLAE. A large number of women, dressed in black, came into Managua and protested outside the special courts, clamouring for hard line judgement to be handed out.

Nora was responsible for the presentation of the charges against the Somocistas. She could also sign the order to release them, without sending them before a judge, 'when we found some merit, some reason.'

At a human level the work of public prosecutor was very difficult for Nora. She remained tender-hearted, concerned about individuals. 'I had before me the dossiers of the National Guard members and I saw their crimes very clearly, but on the other hand I also had the families of those Guard members... The lower level Guardsmen were generally very poor and were the source of income for their family. The woman would arrive, with her swollen belly and her malnourished children, to ask me for clemency... At those moments I wished that the Guard member had no crimes so I could say: Okay, here he is, take him home with you... I remember one pregnant women who planted herself at the entrance to my office very early each

106

morning for a month. She said nothing to me. I already knew. Every day there she was, with her belly and her baby. And the case against her husband was very strong; he was clearly responsible for crimes... I looked for alternatives; I went to the *barrio* to try and get them to help her economically... Finally, I sent the case on to the tribunal. I charged him and they found him guilty. *It was hard, because you had to divide yourself between what you felt and what you had to do.*' (my italics)

Friends and colleagues testify to the emotional stress Nora experienced in this work. Her personal assistant, Guadelupe Romero, talked about how 'all the families came to cry on Nora's shoulder... what to do faced with all that anguish? ... she would go back to check the proof, she didn't want to make a mistake... it affected her a lot, she was so straight, so honest.' (15)

Nora's old student friend Guadelupe Salinas had cause to be thankful for this rectitude. She had been in Chile since 1971 and while she had not taken an active part in the revolution, she hadn't fought against it. 'We came back from Chile after the Triumph, on our way to Mexico. I wanted to show off my two children to my family and friends, but my husband was taken prisoner as a Somocista sympathiser and we had our passports taken off us... I went to see Nora in her capacity as Public Prosecutor - she was working with our old law professor Ernesto Castillo at the time. I knew I was stigmatised so I was feeling quite aggressive, that's my way of reacting...When I walked into the office, she was delighted to see me and came towards me crying out: Lupita! I replied defensively: Here I am. I hope you're not going to bite me! And Nora burst into tears... If it hadn't been for our relationship, my husband would have got a prison sentence. She helped a lot of people like that...'

One problem was, according to Guadelupe Salinas, that the 'old guard' FSLN, those leaders who had been for years in the mountains, only had reference to the thinking of Carlos Fonseca, they were 'less advanced intellectually.' Their viewpoint was quite rigid in some respects and, because of this, many people had been imprisoned unfairly. It was Nora's job to sift out the innocent from the guilty and to transform the rhetoric of revolutionary justice into a reality.

Doña Muriel says: 'The FSLN used her there as well, her rectitude, her nobility. I'm not the only person who believes that. It was such a hard job, judging the Somocistas. But she believed so completely in the cause. And she was always very modest. She never said: I did this, I did that. '

All through this period, there is not one mention of Nora in the newspapers. Despite the fact that she did the actual work, it is Tomás Borge who is remembered as the Sandinista who established an ethos of clemency for the revolution.

The nature of the real crimes that Nora had to present was very disturbing - and she had to go through the cases of about 6000 individual criminals. In particular the extent of the suffering of women under the dictatorship was underlined for Nora throughout the trials. The Guard had had a deliberate strategy of sowing terror in a neighbourhood by indiscriminate rape. Sandinista women were likely to be both raped and killed if they were caught. Systematic rape as a means of torture of prisoners is described by Amada Pineda:

'That night several of them came to where they were holding me. They raped me. I struggled and they began to beat me and that's when they did all those terrible things to me. My legs were black and blue, my thighs, my arms. I had bruises all over me. It was just three days but those three days were like three years to me - three years of being raped by those animals.' (16)

At that time, however, in the newspapers at least, crimes against women were categorised differently. For example, on 11th January 1980 Martinez Castro was described by *Barricada* as being 'responsible for five crimes and a rape.'

On 14th February 1980 Nora was awarded *la Militancia* by the FSLN and nominated as Member of the Sandinista Assembly. She felt very honoured at receiving the award. This at least was a recognition of Nora's services to the revolution and reflected the importance of the public position she held, despite the fact that her name never reached the newspapers.

The new function for women, as announced by an AMNLAE pronouncement made by Doris Tijerino, was to participate in the Sandinista reactivation plan. The newspapers exhorted women to take part in rectifying the destruction caused by Somoza (*adelante mujer con tu participación! ante de la destrucción somocista, la mujer con el plan de reactivación sandinista!*) (17)

Women's involvement at community level had been increasing in many spheres. The new Ministry of Health had begun to set up local health centres in rural areas and *barrios* and to organise health education, vaccination and cleaning campaigns. Of the 78,000 health *brigadistas*, 75% were women. They were given crash courses and then, on specially designated health days, they would pour into their neighbourhoods or walk out into the remote countryside. Vaccinations against infectious diseases such as polio, measles, tetanus and diphtheria, were carried out regularly. Cleaning programmes included rubbish collection; 4,200 latrines were built in the first six months. Health workers flooded people with leaflets on public hygiene and tried to persuade mothers to breast feed in order to reduce problems of infant malnutrition and diarrhoea. Popular Health Councils, the local organising groups, were dominated by women members. Health is a woman's concern when she is responsible for the home and the children - probably the reason why so many women were involved. Even at the time it was noted that men sat back and let the women take the major responsibility for community health care. (18)

Women were equally prominent in the Popular Militias, which were set up to patrol and protect each neighbourhood and provided with basic training in the use of rifles.

In the field of education women's participation was also central. The new Ministry of Education, under Father Fernando Cardenal, had prepared for a crusade with help from Cuban advisors, to carry out Carlos Fonseca's dream, 'to eliminate once and for all the illiteracy which has immersed our people in the most degrading ignorance.'

In March 1980, 100,000 young people set out in a convoy of army trucks, with their new knapsacks containing the literacy primer called 'Sunrise of the People' and a crusade T-shirt, to take part as teachers in the literacy brigades across the country. Sixty per cent of these were young women. And women illiterates were the majority among those to be taught, who now got the opportunity to 'wake up their minds.' (19)

The ethos of the literacy crusade was founded in the educational philosophy of the Brazilian priest Paulo Freire, its aim to involve people in their own learning, to relate their learning to the wider political context and to enable learners to act upon - that is, to change - the world around them. 'It is a cultural action of transformation and growth,' read the introductory notes to the teacher's manual. (20)

After the six month course, Popular Education Collectives (CEPs) were set up by the students themselves, to keep the momentum going. For example, domestic workers (maids) formed three CEPS in one district of Managua alone (las Brisas) - and then these women went on to join the newly established domestic workers' union and to set up a maids' collective in the neighbourhood. (21)

Women also participated in the poetry workshops which had been initiated by the Ministry of Culture, under Father Ernesto Cardenal and Deputy Minister Daisy Zamora. Workshop members met regularly to read and discuss published poetry as well as to write and share their own poems. Not only did the number of women poets increase with the revolution, but they were also permitted to have a sense of humour...(22)

AMNLAE succeeded in putting two new laws through the Council of State. Their first proposal, the Adoption Law, made it legal for single women to adopt fully and also prohibited the export of Nicaraguan children to be adopted abroad. The Law of Breastfeeding banned advertising of powdered milk substitutes.

Next AMNLAE proposed the 'Law between Mothers, Fathers and Children' which would abolish the old automatic status of the man as head of the family (*Patria Potestad*, literally father power) and create equal rights over children for mother and father, whether or not they were legally married. The law stipulated that men were responsible for the children they fathered: paternity, not legally recognised marriage, was the issue (23). This was a very important law in a society with a tradition of consensual unions, fathers away in seasonal agricultural work, men having unions and children with different women, women taking on the economic burden of the family. It reflected the post 1979 concern of the rights and welfare of children.

However women ran into unexpected opposition over the passage of this law. There were heated though trivial discussions about its title - some wanted to retain the term '*patria potestad*' while others argued that the word 'fathers' should precede 'mothers'. All this made it clear that women had a long battle ahead of them in breaking down the embedded ideology of machismo. What was more distressing was that they had to confront men not only from the right-wing political parties but also within the FSLN itself. It took them a year to push this law through.

AMNLAE took responsibility for ensuring new laws didn't discriminate against women. Every Saturday some of the officials would meet to discuss and revise the old legal system, recommending anti-sexist changes law by law. The belief in the potential for radical change is reflected by Milú Vargas who is quoted as saying: 'We have to fight, that's right, we have to accept that. We think we are going to make a revolution inside this revolution. But we have the possibility (here).' (24)

The predominant image of Nicaraguan woman from that time is the lovely longhaired girl suckling her baby and carrying a rifle: it's not a passive image but it does reinforce the concept of the new Madonna - the maternal impulse which nurtures and protects the young revolution. (25)

In general, there was still a process of politicising motherhood by glorifying it rather than politicising women outside their rôle as mothers.

111

Moreover, the focus on women's participation in the productive sphere precluded an analysis of their oppression in the domestic sphere. Yet most women still continued in lower-paying sex-stereotyped jobs and continued to be exclusively responsible for child care and domestic labour. (26) No wonder that many women were not physically able to attend political meetings - even if their partners allowed them!

Amada Pineda is quoted as saying about the situation: 'We are still fighting. And sometimes we have to fight in our own homes. Our husbands want us there, confined within four walls, cooking, washing, ironing, without help from anybody. We must organise to work together to rebuild this wounded country and to fight for our own rights as women...' (27) .

Shortly after the birth of her new baby, Norita José, Nora was nominated to go to Copenhagen as head of the Nicaraguan delegation to the United Nations World Conference on Women, Development and Peace. The aim of the conference, held in July 1980, at the mid point of the United Nations Decade for Women, was to review progress made in the light of the World Plan of Action adopted in Mexico City in 1975.

This was an excellent opportunity for Nora to make contact with women from other countries and to develop her understanding of what was happening in other parts of the world. There was a particular focus on two issues of international concern - the effects of the Israeli occupation on Palestinian women and the effects of apartheid on the status of women in Southern Africa. Nora met representatives of the South West Africa People's Organisation, the African National Congress and the Pan African Congress. The United States supported both the Israeli government and the apartheid régime, that extreme manifestation of the racism that Nora had witnessed in the United States and which had distressed her, as a young student.

The Copenhagen Programme of Action, which was adopted on July 31st by 94 votes to four, called for an increase in the United Nations budget for women, the implementation of women's health and welfare

112

programmes and increased aid to family planning projects. It also requested the United Nations General Assembly to convene an international conference on sanctions against South Africa. The United States, voting against adoption of the programme, expressed their regret over what they described as the politicisation of the conference. (28)

Because of the recent changes in Nicaragua, its progress did not figure much in the review, except for the establishment of the Women's Office in the Ministry of Labour: this was a special programme informing women of their rights in national legislation as well as providing internal co-ordination of projects involving women in development. (29)

As far as developments in Latin America as a whole were concerned, it was recommended that regional organisations such as the Latin American Economic System (SELA) should be involved in identifying and generating economic co-operation projects which affected the position of women. (30) In general, there was concern over the small number of women diplomats involved in regional and inter-regional meetings, the participation of women in these forums being noted as an important factor in change. Additionally, the rôle of national women's organisations in stimulating local networks of women to achieve their economic, social and political needs, was acknowledged. (31)

In early August, Nora flew back to Managua to continue her work in the courts. The special tribunals functioned until February 1981 and then she had the job of closing down the courts. They had heard about 6000 cases and set free some 1300 Somocistas without trial. The largest percentage who were judged were sentenced to five years in prison (around 50%). Around 15% got the maximum sentence of thirty years. Nora followed the progress of those she had accused, commenting in 1987, 'I made mistakes with some of those I gave liberty to... But the majority of those who were condemned to prison and have now been released have gone home to their families, are working and settled back into their lives.' There were still

113

around 2000 Somocista prisoners at that time, but in 'semi-open' prison conditions. (32)

Finally, when her job as Public Prosecutor was over Nora had some personal business to complete. She went to visit Tola, the parish where her great friend from the mountains Gaspar García Laviana had worked and was buried. She took little Alberto with her, the child she had been carrying when she knew Gaspar, and who was now two years old. 'I sat down in the church, and began to imagine him there, in his church, as priest. It's such a pretty church, all whitewashed. Afterwards I went out to visit his grave. And I cried. I don't know how many hours I wept. My son asked Why are you crying, mama? I told him I was crying for a friend who had died and I had not been able to cry until then. And that when a feeling is very strong, it's sometimes hard to find a way to express it. You carry the pain with you and it leaves you only when you can face it.'

Somehow, finally, Nora had managed to come to terms with Gaspar's death, but it had been a long process. She did not feel able to attend the ceremony in Tola where his remains and those of four other comrades were buried in the 'Heroes and Martyrs Park' amid great ovation. Even after Nora's pilgrimage to his grave and the chance to grieve openly, his loss remained deep within her. When she was interviewed for the *Envio* article, years later and a few months before her own death, she is described as 'laughing often and only crying when she recalled Gaspar García Laviana.'

The Foreign Ministry

February 1981 - another Valentine's Day and another move for Nora, into the Foreign Ministry. She was nominated along with Victor Hugo Tinoco, to share the responsibilities of Deputy Minister under the leadership of Padre Miguel d'Escoto, who had been one of the Group of Twelve. Victor Hugo had been at the Nicaraguan Embassy in Washington since the Triumph, where he had been working hard to obtain solidarity and support from international organisations. Now he had the rôle of political deputy while Nora was given an administrative rôle. Nora brought with her from the tribunals her assistant and close friend, Guadelupe Romero.

Victor Hugo suggests several reasons for Nora's nomination to this post: her training as a lawyer, her good command of English but perhaps more than anything her great facility in human communication. While at the beginning she lacked confidence in the political aspect of the job and in public speaking, her capacity for interpersonal relations on a one to one level was already well-known. Therefore she was an excellent choice for all the backstage work that diplomats have to carry out - developing constructive working relationships, lobbying, negotiating, entertaining important guests. (1)

With her customary modesty Nora recalls: 'In this job I felt the weight of the war and above all the weight of my own ignorance. I had no idea about foreign policy, or about diplomacy, I knew nothing about the whole protocol thing or international relations. Nothing!'

While Nora had been focused on bringing to justice the crimes of the past, a new war game had begun. Unfortunately many of the prisoners set free without trial promptly joined the counter-revolution. Already by November 7th 1979 it was being reported that former National Guardsmen had entered Nicaraguan territory from Honduras. (2) Their terrorisation tactics were similar to before, though even more cowardly. There were attacks on farmers and women and children, in remote areas where the counter revolutionaries were safe from immediate reprisals. Village schools and new health centres were burnt to the ground. Volunteer teachers were raped and doctors executed before the terrorists escaped back over the border, taking with them young boys who were brutalised and trained as one of their number. Their target was always to eradicate the social gains of the revolutionary process. (3)

The Carter administration had a public policy of appeasement with regard to relations with the new régime in Nicaragua, wishing to avoid the kind of over-reaction that had occurred with Cuba two decades before and hoping that by being friendly and supplying aid, the US government could moderate the revolutionary process and perhaps eventually defuse it. (2) However, at the same time, the United States began a massive military build-up in the Caribbean. This included the relocation of military manoeuvres normally held on US territory. The aim of this was to erect a *cordon sanitaire* around Nicaragua and to prevent the spread of the revolution to El Salvador and the Caribbean.(5) It also increased the military capacity of some of the smaller islands of the Eastern Caribbean, hoping to develop a conservative pro-US axis in this region.

The United States paid special attention to political and diplomatic relations with Honduras, which was one of the cornerstones of US strategy in Central America, given its key geopolitical position between El Salvador and Nicaragua. It was an ideal base for the infiltration of men and arms to feed conflicts in those neighbouring countries. An invasion force of mercenaries, made up of former members of Somoza's National Guard, anti-Castro Cubans and Guatemalan military personnel, was being secretly trained in Florida under the command of a former member of the United States Special Forces, on directions from the CIA.

In January 1981 Reagan was elected President of the United States and from then on the dominant theme in US-Nicaraguan relations was overt confrontation. The Republican administration was dedicated to removing the Sandinistas from power by whatever means necessary. Nicaragua very quickly became the testing ground for the newly devised

116

doctrine of low-intensity conflict, whereby proxy armies, supported by the United States government through the CIA, would be used to employ guerrilla-style warfare against a country in order to bring the government and the people to their knees. This method, developed as a consequence of the high level of US casualties in Vietnam, precluded the use of US troops or committing large amounts of high-visibility military assistance. The Nicaraguan Democratic Forces (FDN) were established in March 1981 in this way with a membership consisting mainly of ex-National Guardsmen. These counter-revolutionaries came to be known simply as 'the Contra.'

As one researcher put it, 'The White House believed so fervently in its cause (of imposing US hegemony) that it felt compelled to exceed legal, ethical and moral norms of society to achieve its objectives.' (6)

Nora thus joined the Foreign Ministry at a crucial time, to play her rôle in the fight to win international support against this US intervention into Nicaraguan affairs.

Nicaraguan foreign policy was designed to chart an independent course. Painfully aware of their inherent limitations of 'small state actors on the world stage', they decided early on to use international organisations, international law and diplomatic contacts with a wide variety of nations to protect the new political order. (7)

The United Nations system is based on the concept of the equal sovereignty of each state. At regional level, the Charter of the Organisation of American States also specifically prohibited one state's intervention in the internal affairs of another. Furthermore, the Non-Aligned Movement of Third World countries sought to challenge control by the West and to develop a new international economic order. All these organisations provided arenas where Nicaragua could highlight and challenge United States intervention.

'I began my apprenticeship. In reality my whole life has been an apprenticeship. Here I learned from Miguel, from Daniel, from Victor Hugo, from all the other diplomats. And little by little, I grew to enjoy it.

Because I realised that diplomacy is nothing more than constant negotiation; when I was a lawyer, what I liked most was the negotiating part of the job, making contracts.'

In March and April, Nora led the Nicaraguan delegation at the seventh congress of the Latin American Economic System (SELA) in Caracas. And every year in September she was part of the Nicaraguan delegation to the United Nations General Assembly in New York.

Victor Hugo Tinoco had studied medicine in León, after being expelled from the seminary for his left-wing beliefs. He quickly became involved in the Sandinista student movement and went underground in 1976. He fought with Bayardo Arce in the Northern Front where he led a column in the final offensive. He is a tall man, with a thin brown face, black moustache and pointed beard, short tight black hair, long hands that he holds in front of him as he speaks, gesticulating or clasping them together, a man who speaks directly to his audience, with excellent fluent English, not too complicated, not too emphatic, not too rhetorical.

Miguel d'Escoto is short and square: broad shoulders, short moustache, square glasses, square head, balding on top, he leans his weight on his left elbow as he listens, or with his left hand on his hip, motionless, with no facial expression. When he gets up to speak, he spreads his square hands out on the lectern as if it were a pulpit, he raises his hands to emphasise his points, makes them into fists, shakes them. Sometimes he beats the table with his outstretched hand to show approval of another speaker - and occasionally there's a grin, his brown eyes lighting up for a moment. usually, though, a person heavy with his own presence. Miguel came from a very wealthy family and was actually born in the States although he spent his early education in Nicaragua. He had maintained close links with the United States, with the Maryknoll religious community in particular, and these links were very important in providing a range of support for Nicaragua.

Daniel Ortega was a leader of the Insurrectionist Tendency along with his brothers, Humberto (also a member of the National Directorate)

118

and Camilo (who died in combat). His partner was Rosario Murillo, the poet, whom Nora had known since schooldays at the Colegio Teresiano, and with whom Daniel had four children. Daniel was a prototypical revolutionary, both in looks - with a full black moustache, dressed usually in a combat jacket - and in his style of speaking - highly rhetorical, his fist beating the air.

The symbol he took for the election campaign in 1990, 'the fighting cock with his blade unsheathed' - a very sexist image in Nicaragua which was much criticised - unfortunately reflected the strong tradition of machismo of this leader and many of his colleagues. 'The macho rhetoric which felt so good to them was what made them tick... The sheer pleasure they got out of telling the United States: 'Here we are. We won and you can't do a thing about it!', is how Gioconda Belli later described it. However, Gioconda admits, 'we were all guilty of buying into this macho concept of power, of singing hymns to the greatness of our David and Goliath struggle.' (8)

These were the three men Nora travelled with a great deal. Hardly surprising that, even until her death, she felt 'fearful' about speaking in public. It seems she didn't often get the chance to speak at all. Even on issues where she was very involved, it tended to be Miguel or Daniel who actually spoke in the UN Security Council or the UN General Assembly. They had similar political viewpoints and continued to be very close. Even in newspaper reports in the Nicaraguan press, about foreign affairs, Nora's name is rarely found.

The US Ambassador to the United Nations, newly appointed by Reagan in 1981, was Jeane Kirkpatrick, a distinguished academic, previously Professor of Political Science at Georgetown University in Washington where she had worked since 1967. She was, like Reagan, rabidly against the new Nicaraguan goevernment, because of the perceived threat of encroaching Communism in Central America. Her perspective is summed up in the following statement: 'If we are confronted with the choice between offering assistance to a *moderately repressive* (my italics) autocratic government which is also friendly to the United States and permitting it be over-run by a Cuban-trained, Cuban-armed, Cuban-sponsored insurgency, we would assist the moderate autocracy.' (10)

As for Nora, within the Ministry 'everyone loved her and had so much confidence in her' - she quickly became *doctora corazón* (a heart doctor) - a sort of agony aunt. She acted as an informal counsellor, the person everyone would consult for moral support and advice about their personal problems, both men and women. In particular, young women came to Nora for marital advice. 'I try to make them think about what they want to be in life. I ask: 'Do you want to be a whole woman and save your marriage for your kids, or for yourself. Fine, if you're happy and love your husband. Otherwise, there's no sense in being together...You cannot be a parasite for anyone. You may be a beautiful orchid. But you will die and the tree stays.' In the end, though, as Nora said, 'I can listen. But don't expect me to give you the answer. You have to grow up yourself.' (11)

In addition to personal problems, colleagues would also seek Nora out to discuss professional differences or conflicts at work. In this way, as well as through her efficient administration, Nora served in a not untraditional rôle to ensure the Ministry worked together effectively and happily. She was a human leader and she would often be distressed by other people's problems. Her workmates remember, 'Nora did get mad sometimes, too, normally over someone's inefficiency, but she never harboured resentment, she wasn't constantly criticising - once she had expressed her disappointment, it was over.'(12)

'She was accessible, but very firm, very strong - though not inflexible,' remembers Dora Zeledón, who was director of the Asia/Africa/Middle East section. 'There was a comrade who'd carried out something badly and she really flew off the handle about it. But a while later, she called him into her office again and apologised, saying, "I shouldn't have spoken to you like that. Just try to do better next time." She also had that kind of humility, she was aware of her own failings. She had a very positive mixture of characteristics.' (13)

Nora took on responsibility for staff development, particularly with a group of young women who had followed her from the Tribunals. One of these was Consuelo, Guadelupe Romero's sister, who was then about sixteen. 'She formed us, she showed us how to work, how to love, she taught us moral values. I learnt discipline and responsibility from her. I was just a kid, I'd mess around at times. She'd call me in (her office door was always open). Come here you, she'd say and she'd put me on the right road. She created a sense of security for us to work within. And a sense of self-worth. She'd tell us she was depending on us - she couldn't do her job without our contribution.' (14)

This sounds like the sort of supportive training that Oscar Turcios provided for Nora when she was working for him. And, in fact, Consuelo remembers Nora kept a photograph of Oscar in her office, which underlines the importance for Nora of their relationship and Oscar's influence on her development.

'Her office was very personalised,' continues Consuelo, with photos of her children and her mother. She also had a doll collection which grew and grew - she'd bring one back from each country she visited. Her office was quite a contrast to the others - she was the only woman at that level, of course.'

Nora loved to laugh, she laughed a lot - she didn't tell jokes but she would celebrate other people's: 'you could hear that unmistakable laugh of hers throughout the whole ministry,' remembers Victor Hugo. She socialised with her colleagues when she had time; everyone was invited to her birthday party; they all went for an outing to Granada once. 'Whatever space she had, she'd spend with friends. She lived her life intensely, she enjoyed herself openly and frankly,' recalls Dora Zeledón.

Nora also took part on the days when workers were mobilised to carry out some communal task, for example cleaning the streets in one of the poor neighbourhoods. Gloria Tünnerman, who was working in liaison with the United Nations, describes one of these days: 'I remember there was a flood and one of the bottle companies lost all their bottles in the mud. Of course, bottles were very precious then, we didn't throw them away. So we went out in shorts and trainers to dig out the bottles. It was a lot of fun, with your comrades. Nora always joined in when she had time.' (15)

Nora had good relations with everyone, high or low, the fact she was middle class made no difference. She would talk to the cleaning women and the chauffeurs in the same way that she spoke to FSLN leaders ... According to Dora Zeledón, she enjoyed the mobilisation days precisely because she loved to be close to the Nicaraguan people.

Nora had a particular concern for children and she had taken into her household two nieces, the daughters of her sister Lidia Ruby who was then working as a pilot in the Sandinista Air Force. She cared about other people's children too, for all the children of the revolution. Her chauffeur used to tell his grandchildren how Nora hated to see the children selling or begging at the traffic lights. She used to have fierce discussions with him about this, sitting, as she did, up front next to him. 'Are these the cossetted babies of the revolution that Tomás Borge spoke about?'

Once Nora came home from Spain with some clothes as presents for her children. Alberto didn't like the trousers because they had patch pockets and he said he wouldn't wear them. 'That's fine,' retorted Nora. 'If you don't like them, you don't have to wear them. I've got plenty more sons who'll be happy to wear these.'

A final story from Nora's chauffeur recounts how a vehicle attempted to hold them up on the way home from the ministry one night. Nora didn't believe in having bodyguards. 'Don't you worry,' she said, patting his shoulder and pulling a pistol out of her roomy handbag, 'I've got my firearm with me.' (16)

Although her initial job designation reflected a typical division of labour, Nora quickly grew in terms of her political understanding. 'She had to participate in the political analysis,' says Victor Hugo. It seems she had

122

much to thank Victor Hugo for in this aspect of her development. They worked closely together as equals, with mutual respect, being of the same age and having had the same kind of background, firstly in student politics and then in the guerrilla, he having fought on the Northern and she on the Southern Front. They spent a lot of time discussing the political dimension of the work. And usually, because of their shared background, they tended to have a similar political outlook - in contradiction with Padré Miguel, who was older and approached the work from a different viewpoint, from a paternalistic, top-down perspective. 'But this wasn't a bad thing,' recalls Victor Hugo. 'We were able to discuss things and balance each other out. Although, yes, Nora might get mad from time to time about these differences.'

'She took belligerent positions,' says Dora Zeledón,' and we knew her proposals were reflected in the decisions that were taken. Because of the way she was, her competence, her simplicity, she was held in great respect and any suggestion she made would be valued more, both by her superiors and by those who worked to her.'

In November 1981, the Reagan administration authorised US$20 million in military aid to the Contra. But the Nicaraguan leadership, very pragmatically, had begun to take steps to ensure an adequate mechanism of self-defence. The Sandinista Army had already formed new battalions to send to the mountainous zones near the Honduran border. AMNLAE had been asked to provide logistical help, cooking, maintenance tasks, for this initiative and the Committee of Mothers of Heroes and Martyrs was established. The rôle of motherhood was still paramount

A lot of women, having fought alongside men in the struggle, were offended by the suggestion that they were only good for support services and they formed their own battalions to fight in this new war. Although a lot of press coverage was given to their two-week training period, they were not permitted to operate except as reserve battalions. It is interesting to note that many of these women were 'not necessarily young, not necessarily students but rather *compañeras* from the *barrios*, housewives and members of the Sandinista (local) Defence Committees.' (22)

We have here two contrasting views of Nicaraguan women. On the one hand there is the Madonna, who holds her crucified son in her arms, across her lap (and though fully grown, the son is still tiny compared to the mother); on the other there is the defiant warrior, 'my raped girl / standing up and tidying her skirt / going after the murderer following him / uphill and downhill,' as Gioconda Belli describes Nicaragua. (18)

The women's struggle to push through the legal reforms on the family - the law between mothers, fathers and children - continued. After a lengthy process and many heated debates in the Council of State, this was eventually passed in September 1981. (34)

By December 1981 the level of Contra activity had been stepped up considerably, especially on the Atlantic Coast - starting with the 'Red Christmas' raid on North Zelaya. The Contra had support among some of those isolated communities which thus provided a bridge for them into Nicaragua. An army unit was attacked and several Sandinista soldiers were killed. In reprisal, seventeen Miskitos were rounded up and shot at LeimUS. That was reported in *Americas Watch* a few months later.

What they didn't report was that in December 1991 a Contra group kidnapped Dr Mirna Cunningham and a nurse on their way to a house call. The two women were ritualistically raped and beaten, with the soldiers singing Moravian hymns and praying while they abused them. They were brought back to Mirna's home village of Balwaskarma and the entire community turned out to get them set free. However, the incident had destabilised the community and a thousand people crossed the Río Coco to the Miskito camp in Honduras. (20)

Such events led the government to relocate the Miskito Indians from the Río Coco further inland. The intention was to ensure better security but the operation was carried out clumsily, without consultation or explanation. The Sandinista Army moved in and moved whole communities out. The result was that 10,000 Miskitos washed their hands of the new government and fled to Honduras - where they continued to provide a base support for the Contra. The Sandinistas played right into the hands of the CIA in this respect. The United States consistently used the Sandinistas' human rights record on the Atlantic Coast as a weapon against them in international forums.

The propaganda arm of the CIA on the Atlantic Coast was the Moravian Church, who preached a holy war against communism, using hymn books where the words had been radically altered, hymns which the Contra used in ambush and assault. The political formation of MISURATA was due to a Moravian pastor, who was leader of the camps in Honduras, where young Miskitos were being trained for the Contra. (21)

Throughout 1982 Contra activity continued. The FDN bombed Managua airport, killing three civilians. They blew up two of the major bridges in the north, cutting off communications. In September Eden Pastora, who had fought with Nora on the Southern Front and had since then been serving as vice-minister of defence, broke with the revolution and set up another Contra force (ARDE) in Costa Rica, along with Alfonso Robelo who had resigned from the Junta of National Reconstruction in 1980. (22) Nicaragua was now under attack from both north and south. The Sandinista army also fought steadily on the Atlantic Coast against the Contra units.

On 29th September 1982, Nora and Lea Guido attended the fifth anniversary of the Nicaraguan women's movement (taking its starting date from the formation of AMPRONAC in 1977). The celebrations were held in León and Tomás Borge spoke. It was one of those occasions where the spirit rises and rises. Solidarity, common purpose and experience - you can touch it, smell it, hear it. The atmosphere was excitement, wholly benign. Two thousand or more crowded into the hall, thousands more jostled outside to hear the speech - this was the first time a member of the revolutionary government had spoken specifically about women. It was hot, people sweated freely as they waited for the meeting to begin. Tomás spoke brilliantly, presenting a clear marxist analysis, but above all it was his display of integrity, affection and humour that was so convincing.

He honoured the women - the heroines and martyrs of the revolution: 'It's no coincidence that in this city of León the outstanding military leaders were women (*applause*).. Within this constellation there shine Dora María Téllez, Vicky Herrera. And in other parts of the country other women stand out head and shoulders above the men, Doris Tijerino, Gladys Báez.. Women who surely will continue to be active... And here, on this very ground, Luisa Amanda Espinosa shed her blood and the *guerrillera* Arlen Siu left her last song echoing (*applause*)...' (23)

He threatened the men with the Food Law (*la Ley de Alimentos:* this was what they called the legal responsibility of men to contribute to the cost of feeding the children they have fathered). 'And those who don't carry out the law well, here's the Ministry of the Interior to exercise the necessary measures (*applause*) ... Mm I can see some men who aren't applauding with much enthusiasm (*laughter*) ... and some men who aren't applauding at all (*more laughter*) ... and there are some over there who are looking really worried... (*chanting: Let the National Directorate give the order!*) And in this we won't discriminate against colour, hair, size or whatever (*standing ovation*)..'

Tomás gave his support publicly to the new plan for a women's Legal Office and took the opportunity to present a lawyer, 'who is a very important member of the Ministry of the Interior and if the *compañeras* of AMNLAE will accept him, we give him up gladly, so that he can front this office (*applause*).'

He exhorted the crowd to close the gap between the leadership of AMNLAE and the women at the grassroots .... And he left them with great faith for the future. 'A revolution which counts on these women is a revolution which no-one can hold back, which will march on unrestrained towards new dawns... (*applause*)... on their lips the cry of Free Country! (*the people replied: Or Death!*) (*standing ovation*)' (24)

126

In November the US Congress approved another US$24 million in aid to the Contras.

January 1983 was a busy time for Nora. Firstly, she took part in an Extraordinary Meeting of the Co-ordinating Bureau of the Non-Aligned Countries on Latin America and the Caribbean which Nicaragua was successful in convening in Managua. This was a major diplomatic coup as 89 delegations focused their attention on an agenda which was dominated by the Nicaraguan and Central American problems and specifically on the growing number of attacks by the Honduran-based Contra into northern Nicaragua. It set the stage for continued discussion of Central America in the Seventh Summit of the Non-Aligned Movement in New Delhi in March that year.

Nora was also a member of the Nicaraguan group at the United Nations International Court of Justice (the World Court) in The Hague, where they brought a case against the United States for sabotage, with the help of a US law firm, Reichler and Applebaum and of Abram Chayes, a professor at Harvard Law School. She then attended the Latin American Economic Conference in Quito.

That same month saw the birth of a new initiative. Mexico convened a meeting of its foreign minister with those of Colombia, Panama and Venezuela on Contadora island, in the gulf of Panama. The basic concept of the Contadora group was to guide the five Central American countries to a peace agreement amongst themselves that would limit superpower (that is, the United States) intervention in the region. The Contadora initiative was a source of hope because it put in the limelight countries that genuinely wanted to negotiate rather than shoot down negotiations. (25)

Nora was involved with the group from the beginning, as they toured Nicaragua in April that year and subsequently met with representatives of the five Central American countries in Panama City. Contadora activity was maintained over the summer, with meetings in Madrid in May, July and September.

In October 1983, Nora returned to New York with the diplomatic team to lobby the United Nations on behalf of Nicaragua's bid to become a member of the Security Council. The United States, of course, were completely opposed to this and fought a hard ideological battle against Nicaragua's election, proposing instead one of their allies in the region, the Dominican Republic.

Victor Hugo feels that it was particularly thanks to the backstairs lobbying that Nora and Miguel carried out, that Nicaragua was successful, gaining 104 votes - the required two-thirds majority. Nora personally lobbied dozens of crucial Non-Aligned countries under US pressure to vote for anyone but Nicaragua. A colleague in the Ministry, Alejandro Bendaña, agreed later: 'There came a point when we put in our heavy artillery and sent in d'Escoto and Nora, one on one. Nora is warm, friendly and honest. She disarms people. She speaks fluent English and disabuses Americans from the perception that Nicaraguans speak Russian and eat babies for breakfast.' (26)

It was a great victory for Nicaragua to have a place opposite the United States in the Security Council, the key forum of the United Nations dealing with issues of war and peace. Subsequent to this, Victor Hugo spent a lot of time in the United States, involved in the Security Council, and Nora took over many of his political responsibilities. One of these was Contadora. Nora represented Nicaragua in these talks at Deputy-Ministerial level, particularly between November 1983 and April 1984. This was the first stage of the peace process when the preliminary agreement was drawn up and three commissions were also set up to examine security, political and socio-economic issues. She said later, 'The Contadora process appealed very strongly to me... That was a great apprenticeship.'

Nora spoke about representing her country: 'This is a revolution with principles and it bases its foreign policy on its principles. If you have clearly in your mind the principles and interests of your country, it's enough... Because of this you never need to lie, to say one thing when you mean another, to dissemble. I believe there are few diplomats for whom this is possible...

'Marlene Chow said to me, "You have always said just what you thought, the way you wanted to say it. How can you be a diplomat?" The fact is that I've gone on saying what I believe. I've only learned the form in which to say it.'

Diplomacy

In March 1984 Nora was nominated as Ambassador for Nicaragua to the United States. It was a likely choice, given her linguistic and diplomatic skills. The Sandinistas also needed someone they could rely on in this position, from which two ambassadors had already defected. One, Arturo Cruz, had become a Contra supporter.

It has been suggested that Nora's nomination, due to the notoriety centred around her participation in the assassination of *El Perro*, may have been a deliberate ploy on the part of the FSLN to highlight United States involvement in Nicaraguan affairs, to discomfort the Reagan administration and especially the CIA. At this time, the United States were mounting a huge military exercise in the Caribbean, involving 30,000 troops. The mobilisation of troops in Honduras and the number of US ships in the region were 'indications that an invasion could take place at any moment,' according to a Salvadorean observer. (1)

In Nicaragua, preparations had begun for the national elections, one of the conditions imposed by the United States on the Contadora peace process. Daniel Ortega was in New York at the Security Council, having convened a special meeting to highlight the threat to Nicaragua's security posed by illegal US military intervention, while the United States House of Representatives was debating a new aid package to the Contra. The United Nations International Court of Justice in The Hague had censured the United States for mining the Nicaraguan ports. Miskitos had been kidnapped by Contra on the Atlantic Coast. Sandinista defence mechanisms were being stepped up, including the formation of new battalions through conscription and a call for volunteers from the cities to help in the coffee harvest and other production brigades. (2)

In this context, 'the nomination of Astorga seemed to take Washington by surprise and struck many as a direct challenge to the White House,' said a US State Department representative as reported in *Time Magazine*. 'Nicaragua took a real chance sending us someone so notorious.' Normally a nomination follows a discreet routine of evaluation by the State Department and formal recommendation by the President. 'But Astorga's nomination was far from typical and had already attracted too much public attention to be reviewed behind closed doors.' (3)

Although press accounts of the assassination revel in the seduction scene, they also pick up the crux of the matter - the relationship between General Vega and the CIA. One report on the day of Nora's nomination says, 'The rumour circulating here (Managua) is that General Vega was a member of the CIA and the CIA has said it would be unacceptable to allow someone who is responsible for the murder of one of their officers to become Ambassador to the United States.' (4) On the other hand, some State Department officers argued that the nomination ought to go through rather than give the Sandinistas a chance to retaliate by declaring the newly appointed US Ambassador to Nicaragua, Harold Bergold, *persona non grata.*

The outgoing ambassador, Anthony C. E. Quainton, met with Victor Hugo Tinoco several times to urge the withdrawal of Nora's nomination. This request was denied because, according to Tinoco, Nora was regarded as well qualified for the post and the Nicaraguan government truly hoped that she would improve communications.(5)

Whether the nomination was a Sandinista ploy to embarrass the United States regime or not, the House of Representatives voted US$21 million to the Contra on 6th April. At the Contadora talks on 9th April in Panama City, there was a increased open presence of foreign troops, US advisors and US weapons. Several members of Congress complained about direct CIA participation in the attacks on Nicaraguan ports. Reagan's policy was widely criticised.

Several weeks elapsed before the US administration finally turned down the nomination. But Nora's public image as the Mata Hari of the revolution was established by the media during that time. One diplomat wryly observed that Nora was a 'hostess with unusual experience,' adding, 'There's a limit to how close I'd get to her.'(6)

131

Nora, by contrast, said rather tartly: 'I only remember (the assassination) when journalists remind me of it!'

Phyllis Rose, a professor of English at Wesleyan University in the United States, provided a feminist analysis of the significance of the assassination and its basis for the US rejection of Nora's nomination. In a highly plausible explanation for the obsession of the press with this aspect of Nora's past, she wrote:

'How you feel about it (political murder) tends to depend on two things: how long ago it happened and whether you agree with the killer's politics. Political murder may be more than usually problematic when a woman is implicated. Two crimes are being committed - a murder and a betrayal of expectations about female behaviour... Having played on notions of what a woman should be like (that is, harmless and passive) in order to disarm the enemy, the revolutionary heroine involved in murder defies our notions of what a woman is. She uses female stereotypes to succeed and in succeeding overthrows the stereotypes.

'A Freudian would say we are fascinated with female assassins because they represent men's deepest fears. Men go into sexual encounters assuming the harmlessness and passivity of their partners. As we also know from Freud, the things we fear most we tend to joke about most. Perhaps this explains the extraordinary levity with which the American press has tended to treat the appointment of Nora Astorga. I wonder if a male version of Nora Astorga - a former revolutionary terrorist appointed Ambassador to the United States - would be treated with such levity.'(7)

There is also a parallel between sexism at an individual level and the relationship between the United States and Nicaragua. The United States was a large powerful nation throwing its weight against a small backward 'banana republic,' which was expected to be harmless and passive and yet had dared to behave contrary to stereotype. As Nora herself put it in an interview with Art Harris of *The Washington Post*, 'The United States treats undeveloped countries like little children. Their attitude is: If you behave, I'll give you some candy. If not, I'll spank you.'

Nora seems to have been surprised by the US reaction to her nomination. According to *Newsweek*, it was Nora herself who announced to the press at the beginning of March that she had been nominated and that they 'were awaiting an answer from the State Department.' (8) On March 20th she confirmed at Sandino International Airport that she was to be appointed the new Nicaraguan ambassador to the United States in the next four weeks 'once the administration gives the approval.' (9) According to Carlos Tünnermann, Nora was 'on her way' to Washington by the time the rejection came. She didn't seem to expect her nomination to be contested.

Despite this rejected nomination, Nora continued to maintain a high profile in the male-dominated world of diplomacy. In September 1984 it was she who led the Nicaraguan delegation to the United Nations General Assembly in New York. Daniel Ortega came up to make a blistering attack against Reagan in the General Assembly and had a busy schedule in front of television cameras, at network lunches and elegant soirées with businessmen, as well as dinner with the Contadora Ministers.

In his article Art Harris observed that Nora often accompanied Ortega and 'usually winds up running the show'. She had certainly become an object of great interest since the press reporting earlier that year and particularly, it seemed, to women, because of the way she had overturned the stereotypes. Susan Horowitz, a political activist, was quoted in the article as saying Nora was 'an inspiration for the New Woman, she's the most exciting modern female revolutionary around.' Although Nora tried to keep out of the limelight, it was difficult for her not to upstage her colleagues - since she was the one people wanted to meet.

In October Nora was featured on Mike Wallace's popular show *Sixty Minutes* as well as giving the interview to Art Harris. 'None of the Sandinistas sought personal interviews,' claims Donald J Casey, who acted as a media advisor to the Nicaraguan government, 'but sometimes we would advise them to, if we felt it would be influential.' (10)

In fact, Don Casey admits that 'we should have had more control' over the interview with Art Harris. Nora agreed to meet him at the house where the Nicaraguan Ambassador to the United Nations lived. Maybe because she felt relaxed here, she spoke with an unfortunate lack of caution. Asked yet again about the General's assassination, Nora - still claiming this as a revolutionary act and never wishing to deny her part in it - compared herself to Judith of biblical fame who murdered King Holofernes after he subjugated the Jews. Harris developed this analogy into a paragraph of weird psycho-journalism which reveals more about him than it does about Nora:

'The allusion to Judith evokes the incredible horror of a man's betrayal by woman. Classical paintings conjure the parable with gory scenes of Judith holding a severed head aloft, dripping blood, mocking man's weakness and raising the ultimate question: Is all fair in love and war? And is it fair for a woman to fight on both battlefields at once?'

In November Nora was head of the delegation to the Fourteenth General Assembly of the Organisation of American States, held in Brazil, an event characterised by tensions between the United States and Nicaragua, as reported in the press. Secretary of State George Schultz talked about the 'dangerous military imbalance' in Central America, while Nora strongly criticised US policy towards her country. (11) She claimed that the United States were looking for the right moment and the political excuse to invade Nicaragua and that international public opinion was being prepared for this. She also accused the US administration of 'torpedoing' the activities of the Contadora group, by pressing its Central American allies to propose substantive changes to the group's draft peace plan. This had been signed by Nicaragua back in September but in October the three other countries had presented an entirely new draft. (12)

Meanwhile, on the 4th November, the FSLN won 64% of the seats in the National Assembly and Daniel Ortega was elected President and Sergio

Ramírez Deputy-President, with 67% of the vote. They were officially sworn in at the beginning of 1985.

The fortunes of Nora's female comrades were mixed. Rosario Murillo, common-law partner to Daniel Ortega, featured favourably in a press report in *The Houston Post* at this time. She herself had been elected as a deputy to the new 90-member National Assembly and was the general secretary of the Nicaraguan Writers Union as well as the Sandinista Cultural Workers Association. She was reported as 'one tough political organiser and an elegant spokesperson in pleading her country's case' (13). Others were less happy, as appears clearly in Margaret Randall's interviews with many of these women in 1994. (14)

As Deputy Minister of Culture, Daisy Zamora came into conflict with Rosario Murillo, who wished to be seen as the leader of the cultural community. Daisy had also refused to fall in with last minute autocratic demands from the new President to cancel public performances so that visiting artists could entertain the National Directorate in private. She made enemies and was finally forced out of her post.

Michèle Najlis had been removed from her post in charge of immigration by Tomás Borge because he didn't like to be criticised. When she argued with him and questioned decisions that were made, he claimed that 'women never understand these things', and later that, 'she has an identity problem: the woman's crazy.' In addition to the mistreatment and humiliation she experienced, he refused to release her from the Ministry. She was stuck answering the phone. In desperation she finally got Omar Cabezas, the Deputy Minister, to release her ('or arrest me as a deserter').

Gioconda Belli had been responsible for the FSLN election campaign. She recalled, 'I did the work but when it came to naming the person in charge, of course they chose a man. I really fought that; I was furious. Their response was simply that "this is a sexist society."'

Daisy Zamora feels that more women with prestige should have spoken out. However, Doris Tijerino has a different position: 'Let's face it, the FSLN haven't really had a policy of promoting women to leadership positions. Women who have reached those levels have done so at enormous personal sacrifice...' She recalls the patronising speech made by one of the *comandantes* when she was named Chief of the National Police and the tart reply she had made, in public : 'I asked him if after twenty years of revolutionary militancy, they'd just discovered I could think! They said I was difficult, that it was hard to work with me because I came out and said things like that... I had to make a huge effort not to let bitterness get the better of me. My Party history won me authority and respect at the Ministry of the Interior, but I had serious problems with the male leadership. All the female comrades did.'

A second important issue for the women in post-Triumph Nicaragua was sexual harassment. Daisy Zamora was pursued by one of the *comandantes* (she won't say which), who, among other things, suggested her for the post of Deputy Minister in Foreign Relations. When she declined the sexual privileges which went with this position, the *comandante* blocked her from finding other work as well as hampering the career of her new partner. Her perception is that some women didn't decline in these circumstances. 'The quickest and easiest way for political women to acquire a 'protector' and gain direct access to power was by sleeping with someone in power.'

Gioconda Belli spoke at the time about the opposite problem for the professional woman. 'The man sees her as an equal and therefore not as a woman. A woman who has freed herself may have excellent men friends, close relationships, *compañeros* who tell her their troubles, who confide in her and share many things with her, but it never occurs to him to think of her as a possible companion. The minute that idea comes up, they begin to back off. They can't deal with it. They don't yet know how to overcome their fear of a woman who is their equal'. (15)

In contrast to the experience of other women at this time, Nora was perhaps lucky that she had ended up in a workplace where there were no personal differences between her and her superior, nor other internal enemies. According to those who knew her at the time, Nora obviously enjoyed great support from all her immediate colleagues. In addition, she had an important job in which she increasingly showed her diplomatic and political capacity - she continued to develop. Minister Miguel d'Escoto had the highest regard for Nora's abilities and continued to give her greater responsibility. Victor Hugo Tinoco feels that her human persona was so evident, so public, that it would have been impossible to marginalise her. Everyone loved her, from subordinates in the Ministry to political enemies at the United Nations.

'Nora shone,' says Consuelo Romero, then one of the younger secretaries in the Ministry. 'When Nora entered the room, everybody separated in order to greet her. All the ambassadors wanted to know her.' (86)

However, Nora had to work hard to establish equal participation. Even after Victor Hugo returned to Managua, when they were really sharing the political rôle, Victor Hugo admits, 'she didn't always participate in political decisions.... Her fundamental contribution was to give to the revolution a human face abroad, really a feminine face, a softer face. She was able to communicate the message of the revolution without shocking people... she made the revolution more acceptable.' In some respects, Nora was again fulfilling the rôle that young attractive middle class women had played before the Triumph, in publicity and propaganda work abroad.

Guadelupe Salinas also indicates that Nora's position was not so easy. 'Nora was always treated with respect, she succeeded in winning recognition from the National Directorate. But she had to fight against becoming woman-as-object. In her work she had to confront machismo, and sometimes she would come home and cry. Why? because she lived in a *machista* society with all those double standards and she had to cope with it ... problems with men at work, trying to minimise her profile, not giving her the responsibility she deserved because she was a woman. But (fortunately) she was very realistic ... and she had a firmness, she could be

137

very hard in certain situations. And I'm not saying she didn't suffer from sexual harassment from time to time - but Nora had her space (Guadelupe draws a square around herself) and that was that.'

Somehow Nora kept men at a sufficient distance to maintain herself as 'woman-as-subject' both personally and politically. Guadelupe adds, 'She was a person with great conviction, ready to fight against social effects.' She was still the eternal conspirator, playing a rôle at work, as she had when she was keeping *El Perro* at arm's length, willing to adapt in her public performance, in order to achieve what she wanted for Nicaragua, but without betraying her underlying principles.

There were also conflicts in Nora's personal life. Both she and Chester were working very hard in different 'trenches'. They didn't have much time together and neither did they have much time with their children. Everyone attests to the fact that Nora adored her children and that her home was a happy one, they had a lot of fun together. Her mother lived with them and looked after the children when Nora was away - since she travelled a lot with her work.

Like many revolutionaries she sacrificed her family life, Dora Zeledón feels. She didn't have much time with her children, but her priority was safeguarding the revolution. According to Chester, 'After Norita was born, Nora's workload intensified, she had a fanatical interest in her work. I told her the family should have equal importance. I couldn't accept a revolution in which it was necessary to neglect your children; otherwise you just have a revolution in the abstract. But she wouldn't agree. So in the end, we separated. She said I was machista.'

Guadelupe feels there was another side to the situation. 'Nora's relationship with Chester was different to that she had with Jorgé. He was more mature, there was more communication between them. But there you are, a woman in the public eye is attractive and yet it is that which causes problems too.'

138

Despite their eventual split, the evidence is that Nora and Chester loved each other very much: 'I had enormous respect for her. We never had any serious disagreements (apart from this one) and we used to pull each other's leg all the time,' Chester remembers.

'She didn't need him,' says Doña Muriel, with her continuing admiration for her daughter, 'She was so capable.' Yet Lea Guido remembers that separation was not as easy as Nora herself might make out publicly. (She was reported as saying, 'With a revolution and kids, you don't have much time for a husband.' (16)). After the Triumph, Lea and Nora would meet up once a week, on Wednesdays, to provide mutual support. 'We'd talk about problems with our kids, how we didn't have enough time with them; about our feelings of loneliness, our relationships with men - we had similar experiences, a similar viewpoint - neither of us had ever found the one true partner that we had hoped for. It was hard, sometimes, keeping your sense of self-esteem. We'd argue about which one of us was sadder than the other.'(17)

The women's movement within Nicaragua was increasingly affected by the war effort. While women took on greater responsibility for production after conscription, thereby developing non-traditional work skills, the emphasis was still on their being the mothers of the revolution, providing moral and logistical support and a key information network.

Back in 1983 when conscription was introduced, there had been another fierce debate in the Council of State with AMNLAE's representative arguing at length for women's military participation. Although provisions were written into the law allowing women volunteers, the first women were not accepted until early 1986 - and then in explicitly non-combat positions. (18) At the time AMNLAE conceded the (male) FSLN position, given the war situation and the perceived necessity of maintaining unity within the party.

Doris Tijerino later said to Margaret Randall, 'We can see now that it was a mistake to maintain the subordination of AMNLAE... but in those

139

days if a woman with a leadership position in AMNLAE was a party member, she would naturally continue to operate out of party discipline...'

When Dora María Téllez was made Minister of Health in 1985, debates about women's rights continued. One was the issue of contraception. Over half the population was under five and the birthrate was rising. Even though contraception was available in health centres, with donations from abroad, the supplies were going to waste. Women's discussions at the grassroots had highlighted the need for an integrated programme of family planning to be implemented, but this was difficult to achieve. Some women speculated this was because of fear of eliciting yet another backlash from the established Catholic church, while others pointed to the lack of understanding on the part of some of the men in key positions. (19)

Even more problematic was the issue of abortion. *MADRE Speaks* reported on the positions expressed. 'Abortion is a social trauma,' Dora María told the MADRE delegation to Managua in 1985. 'And, of course, when you prohibit abortion, you protect those who can pay... the poor are the ones who suffer.'

Daniel Ortega's response to these concerns was, 'Abortion is one of those exotic ideas imported from Europe and the United States. It's something only intellectuals are concerned with, it doesn't have any relevance to the lives of ordinary people.'

'Two hundred and fifty women a year die of botched abortions in this hospital alone,' doctors from the Hospital Bertha Calderón told him in one of the public meetings held at this time. 'It's intellectual claptrap,' repeated Daniel. 'Like this notion of family planning...The duty of women is to reproduce, the war is killing our combatants, we need more children.' (20) Dora María called on AMNLAE to help inform women about the existing contraceptive programme the Ministry of Health had available. But AMNLAE was too involved in the war effort.

Nevertheless Dora María, along with prominent women doctors, psychologists and journalists, did succeed in setting up a sex education programme which was conducted partly through the media, especially radio and television, reaching a broad-based audience.

Apart from the early influence of the sisters of the Colegio Teresiano, it is noticeable that Nora speaks publicly only about the influence of men in her life, rather than her relationship with women. She doesn't speak about her deep friendship with Lea Guido, for example, or about her involvement with AMNLAE. For she did manage to keep her links with AMNLAE, she attended all the annual conferences and would have passionate discussions about the women's movement.

'But it was an effect of the rôle she played,' explains Guadelupe Salinas, 'that she lost touch with a lot of her friends because she was so much in public life... In her tiny free spaces, we might keep in touch... And that rôle, those tasks, didn't allow her to integrate into the women's movement (as much as she would have liked). But she always represented, accentuated a space for women, she had a lot of presence in the women's movement because of her public profile, even though she was involved in structural transformation of a different kind. She was able to be a leader without losing her femininity ... And, somehow, she managed to neutralise, to overcome the envy of other women... '

Perhaps women perceived that Nora was acting autonomously, that she kept faith with her own beliefs, that she had her own space and that her interest was for others rather than for herself. It may be that this commitment to the task was one reason why Nora didn't appear much in the press within Nicaragua - public recognition was not important to her and she was not ambitious for political power. What many people emphasise is Nora's objectivity, her clarity of vision, her capacity to see right from wrong. 'She was super-intelligent,' says Chester.

According to Dora Zeledón Nora also actively supported women in the workplace. She had a special concern for the promotion of women into decision-making positions. 'If she saw a competent objective woman, she would nominate her for promotion and she succeeded in helping other women get to the top.'

Consuelo Romero remembers how Nora called her into her office and told her she had nominated her to work as Miguel d'Escoto's personal assistant. 'I was terrified. I'd heard the Father could be very difficult to work with and there were a lot of confidential papers that I would have to deal with. I said I didn't want to do the job. Nora replied that it was a revolutionary order. And actually I admitted to her much later that I never had a single problem with the Father. "You see, I told you you could do it," Nora said.'

Press coverage outside Nicaragua was usually negative at this stage. In April 1985 Nora toured the United States with Daniel in a public relations drive, hoping to influence the forthcoming Congressional vote on aid to the Contra. The tour was supported by members of the Democratic Party such as Edward Boland and Chris Dodd. 'Sandinistas Pin Hopes on Congress' was a *New York Times* headline.

The *National Review* reflects the kind of reporting that US citizens were subjected to on Nicaragua. The Sandinistas are referred to as 'a brutalitarian puppet government' and Nora is referred to only in the article as 'Ortega's deputy foreign minister, Nora Astorga, the former seductress and killer.' (21)

Nora worked so hard that her health suffered. She would stay in the office until late at night, perfectionist as she was, and suffered migraines as a result. She seemed to exist on coffee and cigarettes, chain smoking ('she smoked like crazy' is how more than one person described her) and, despite her slim figure, watching her weight. She used to work out regularly in the gymnasium to keep fit.

But there was something more serious. Nora rang Chester one night and asked to meet him. 'I picked her up from the Ministry and we went to a restaurant. I could see she was worried. She told me she'd discovered a lump in her breast. "What do you think I should do?" she asked. "Well, you're the witchdoctor," I reminded her, joking as we always did with each other. "You've got to get a check-up."

'She told me that she couldn't because she had to go away for four months. (The schedule included a meeting of the Non-Aligned Movement in New Delhi to discuss Namibia and then the United Nations Conference on Women in Kenya.) I said, "No you don't. And anyway what about the children, you need to be here for them."' Then they began to argue about this issue again and Chester lost his temper.

Nora went on the trip anyway. Miguel d'Escoto recalls the visit to New Delhi in April 1985. 'She told me she wasn't feeling well and so we began her treatment. There were various medical examinations, coming at shorter and shorter intervals...' (22)

When she returned from India, she rang Lea Guido saying, 'Hey *negra* (black woman - Nora always called her that), I have something to tell you.' Lea remembered, 'We met up. But, to tell the truth, after that I was never able to talk about the cancer with Nora, it was too hard for me. And she always acted as if there was nothing wrong, as if there was nothing there.' (23)

'Maybe if she'd had the mastectomy in time, instead of going away, things might have been different,' says Doña Muriel. 'But she only thought of the revolution.'

Although she was less involved in the women's movement at national level, Nora did represent Nicaragua internationally on women's issues. She attended the United Nations World Conference to review and appraise the United Nations Decade for Women, held in Nairobi from July 15th to 27th that year, again as leader of the Nicaraguan delegation. Nora subsequently had full powers to sign the Convention on Women's Nationality in New York.

The Convention on the Nationality of Married Women, which was brought into force in August 1988, protects the right of women to a

143

nationality of their own. Under this convention 'each contracting state agrees that neither the celebration nor dissolution of a marriage between one of its nationals and an alien, nor the change of nationality by the husband during the marriage, shall automatically affect the nationality of the wife.'

International political issues in fact were debated at length during the conference and several delegations made criticisms of US foreign policy, among the most critical being the Soviet delegation (led by Valentina Tereshkova, the first woman astronaut), the Nicaraguan and Syrian delegations and the representatives of the African National Congress.

It was agreed that obstacles to the advancement of women included war, apartheid, racism and imperialism. Only the United States voted against the paragraph on apartheid, which called for an end to collaboration with South Africa. (24)

As well as diplomacy, Nora learnt other things from Father Miguel d'Escoto. She herself had long separated from the Church, although her ambivalence towards religion is reflected in the fact that she was bringing up her household of children as practising Catholics. 'Her relationship with Miguel was more distant (than hers with me), because of his age, his seniority,' remembers Victor Hugo. 'Maybe her relationship with him did have a religious aspect. Miguel was the synthesis of revolutionary commitment and religious (spiritual) life. Maybe he did help Nora to reconcile those two beliefs within herself, to realise that she did still believe in God...' 'Miguel regarded Nora like a daughter and they spent hours talking together,' said Consuelo Romero.

There had long been a split between the revolutionary priests and the established Church hierarchy. The aim of the Pope's visit to Nicaragua in March 1983 was to criticise the priests in government and to bolster the counter-revolution . Obando y Bravo was made cardinal in 1985, the only one in Central America, and on his return home from Rome, celebrated a mass in Miami for Contra leaders. Obando came to be known as the ambassador of the counter-revolution. (25)

The commitment of the revolutionary priests was in sharp contrast. But Miguel d'Escoto used his position as a priest to produce some publicity of his own. In 1985 he began a fast in the parish church of Monseñor Lescano in Managua, which lasted for forty days. The fast made an enormous impact on all sectors of the country and received international coverage. The following year Miguel d'Escoto launched the Way of the Cross for Peace and Life on the first Friday in Lent. He set out from Jalapa on a 14 day march to Managua with 100 Christians. Those disabled by the war led the march in their wheelchairs. Thousands of people joined the procession for part of the way. Miguel announced: 'We have become convinced that this is the time to act, to carry out profoundly significant prophetic actions in face of the war imposed on Nicaragua.' (26)

Nora said, 'I learned to separate the Church from its representatives. Unfortunately they have an influence that can separate you from everything you believe, and you can end up believing that faith is a mere formula, that at its foundation there is nothing. I have finally come to understand that my break (with the Church) was not a rupture in my faith in God, because that is something very personal... And that I owe, above all, to Miguel, because he helped me restate my faith, he along with a group of priests that were committed.'

In November 1985 Nora spoke in the United Nations General Assembly against Washington's policy of backing mercenary forces. 'The United States have not only created a mercenary army that it trains, finances, advises and directs, but they also expect us to recognise it as a legitimate counterpart for resolving "the Nicaraguan problem"'. In response to the assurance that equipment delivered to the Contra by the United States, such as helicopters and trucks, would not be used for military purposes, Nora retorted: 'What could it be for, then? Could it be that the mercenaries are going to devote themselves to tourism in Central America?' (27)

145

The following day, there was an announcement in Honduras of the next United States-Honduras joint military manoeuvres, as preparation for a possible direct intervention.

In December 1985 Nora was designated head of the Nicaraguan delegation to the Fifteenth General Assembly of the Organisation of American States, to be held in Cartagena, Colombia. She was also due to attend the Eleventh Congress of SELA immediately afterwards in Caracas.

The United States was doing its best to sabotage the second Contadora agreement. The draft resolution, calling for direct negotiations between Nicaragua and the United States and an end to all military manoeuvres by external powers in the region, had been submitted to the United Nations General Assembly by the Contadora group with the sponsorship of the Lima group. (28) And the plan was to endorse it at the OAS Assembly. The United States tried to persuade Panama, Venezuela and Colombia to withdraw the draft. But somehow Mexico managed to influence a change of mind and persuaded them to support it.

Secretary of State George Schultz arrived in Cartagena for a one-day visit to make it clear that the United States would continue to support the mercenaries indefinitely, even if all the Central American countries signed the Contadora Act. The United States had no intention of resuming direct negotiations with Nicaragua. On the same day, one of the Sandinista army helicopters was shot down by a surface to air missile of the SAM-7 type. (29) A message was sent from Managua informing the Organisation of American States that Nicaragua would not attend the General Assembly.

The following day the representatives of Honduras, El Salvador and Costa Rica announced they would not endorse the draft. Nora flew out to Cartagena the same day, presumably on orders from the leadership, to make the Nicaraguan presence felt . She boycotted the further meeting of the Contadora Group and the other Central American countries, held next day, and instead gave a press conference: 'The Contadora Group should give priority to ending the US aggression toward Nicaragua. Without an agreement between the United States and Nicaragua, the rest has absolutely no importance.' (30)

New governments were due to take office in Guatemala and Honduras in January and Costa Rica in April, which may mean a change in policy towards the negotiations: Nicaragua (Nora) requested suspension of negotiations for five months. This was announced at the end of the OAS Assembly by the Colombian Foreign Minister Augusto Ocampo who commented that: 'the United States and Nicaragua are in deep confrontation which damages and deteriorates the process of negotiation.' (31)

Letters had been sent, during Nora's absence, by Daniel Ortega and Victor Hugo Tinoco to George Schultz himself and to Edgardo Paz Barnica, the Minister of Foreign Affairs for Honduras, protesting against the aggression and calling on the Contadora group to take direct steps to persuade the United States to change its policy towards Nicaragua.

But they had an additional strategy for influencing events on the world stage...

The United Nations

Nora was nominated to the post of permanent representative for Nicaragua to the United Nations in January 1986. 'The hardest part was to think that I would have to live outside Nicaragua. I said to Miguel, "Look, I'm like one of those tall trees that have roots deep in the earth; if you pull them up and transplant them to a different environment, you make them shrivel up." "No, you'll see, you won't shrivel up," was his reply. Nicaragua is a country in which you live constantly in contact with reality,' she went on to explain. 'In the United States that just isn't the case.'

Dora María Téllez, Minister for Health, summed up the difference as follows, 'New York is a neurosis assembly plant while Nicaragua is a mental health factory.' (1)

However, this is some kind of an attempt on Nora's part at hiding the other reality: her own illness. Despite being diagnosed with cancer, she took up the post of Ambassador to the United Nations, presenting her credentials to Secretary General Javier Pérez de Cuellar of Peru on 11th March 1986. At the press conference that followed, Nora denied the allegation that Nicaragua was seeking to export revolution to other countries with her unique combination of humour and logic. 'Revolutions are not exportable like Coca-cola or paperbacks... Revolutions are made in a country when the conditions in that country are for a process of change.'

Nora still suffered from the *femme fatale* image. She told a UN friend that the stares she encountered when she took up the post made her feel like a collector's item, a museum piece. (2)

Back home, during March, there was a series of combats along the Nicaraguan-Honduran border, which were probably the most intense of the entire war with the counter-revolutionaries and which confirmed their decline. The Nicaraguan Army announced the Contra forces had suffered 600 casualties, including 350 deaths; they also announced the destruction of a number of their camps attached to the most important Contra training base on the Honduran border.

When the Reagan Administration accused Nicaragua of invading Honduras, Nora called press conferences and went on US national television to charge the Administration with 'lies and fabrications.' The Nicaraguan position was quite clear. Their fight was with the Contras, it was not an act of aggression against Honduras - even though, of course, Honduras was supporting the Contra cause by allowing them to keep their bases on Honduran territory (not to mention the fact that Contra training was carried out with help from the CIA and the forces kept going though US funding).

However, nobody in the press believed Nora, and this Honduran affair was quoted as one of the instances where not 'even the most sophisticated media campaigns can help Ms Astorga to defend some of Nicaragua's positions.' (3)

The four children, Muriel now about fourteen and baby Norita almost six, had packed up and accompanied Nora to New York. If Nora had to be away from Nicaragua, she didn't want to be away from her family. She also took her own cook and chauffeur from Managua. Like her predecessor, she found a house to rent by a river in a leafy area of Scarsdale, a smart suburb north of Manhattan, and the children went to the local (prestigious) public schools.

Very soon Nora rang her mother in Nicaragua asking her to come and live with them. 'She needed me, the schedule was so tiring, she couldn't cope,' said Doña Muriel.

Nora's young cousin was part of the household as were Lidia Ruby's two daughters. Roberto Carlo came up in the holidays. Nora had also requested that her long-time friend and personal assistant, Guadelupe Romero, accompany her to the United Nations. 'But her husband didn't want her to go to New York,' explains her sister Consuelo. At least she visited every holiday, 'Nora insisted that she did.'

149

Unfortunately at this time a serious rift developed between Nora and Chester. Chester was still working at the Ministry, in administration, and disagreed with the direction that foreign policy was taking. He not only left the Ministry over this disagreement, he also left the country, going to Costa Rica. 'I just left,' he said, 'There were infidelities, immoralities on the part of the FSLN leadership... injustices, a kind of disrespect for the people, which I couldn't accept, not after all that time I had fought for something different... I was criticised very badly for leaving, but they never asked, "What's wrong?"'

Nora would accept no criticism of the National Directorate. According to Chester, 'Despite her own rectitude, she was unable to see their corruption. They know what they're doing," she'd say. They were a deity to her and their pronouncements were the words of God. It was a religious passion with her, something to do with her Christian upbringing. Despite her otherwise clear vision, she didn't recognise her own fanaticism.'

Victor Hugo felt that Nora cried more over Chester's defection, specifically because it was a political difference which had finally separated her from him, rather than a personal difference. And Nora was so upset that she severed relations with Chester while she was in New York, up to the point where she didn't allow him to speak to their children by phone.

Soon after she arrived in New York Nora took part as a guest speaker in the 120th anniversary celebration of the magazine *The Nation*, along with Jesse Jackson, Bella Abzug, Molly Irvins, Ira Glasser and Studs Terkel. With over three thousand people, the place was crowded, 'the suspension was roisterous, the speeches were stirring... The scene was set by a powerful sense of the past... But the night was filled with a remarkable feeling for the future as well... The speakers looked ahead to the world (we) will face, into the next century.' (4)

Nora moved in the same circles as Dr Carlos Tünnerman, who had been sent there as Ambassador to the United States in her place when the Reagan administration refused her diplomatic permission. 'But they couldn't stop her becoming Ambassador to the United Nations,' Carlos observed. Although he was more involved with the White House, they were together in other forums, went on visits and arranged tours for Daniel Ortega together, liaising regularly with Agendas International, the media advisory firm. (5)

In May 1986 it happened that Carlos Tünnermann was in Cuba when Nora flew down to la Havana again for more tests. Carlos and his brother Guillermo were there with their mother who was in the same hospital, in intensive care, about to die. This is how he describes the situation:

'Nora was diagnosed with cancer and they operated on her. (She finally had a double mastectomy).They were proposing various treatments but she said: "I've got so many things to do." The cancer had passed from the breast into the lymphatic system and she knew it was incurable. There was a new treatment in Cuba but she said she didn't have the time. She decided the best thing was to opt for chemotherapy; she was in the clinic for three or four days, because it takes it out of you. Before I left, I visited Fidel Castro. He told me (I knew he was referring to Nora but he didn't mention her name because he respected her decision to choose the other treatment) about this marvellous new treatment they had and that they were willing to do anything to help a friend. I passed this on to Nora but she said that the treatment would take three or four months - it just wasn't possible.'

Nora did not want to waste time on treatment that she believed would not cure her; she preferred to spend the time she had left fighting the United States on the world stage and, in doing this, she fought the cancer off for more than 18 months longer. As Lea Guido says: 'She really didn't believe that she'd die so quickly, despite everything... and she continued to smoke!!' (6)

However, after leaving Cuba, she did spend a short holiday in the Corn Islands, fifty kilometres off the Atlantic Coast. This is a small paradise of tranquillity, surrounded by the warm blue Caribbean Sea, lined with white palm-fringed beaches. It is divided in half by the airstrip, along which the island used to come alive at night. Several bars, with huge empty dance floors and jukeboxes belting out loud suspension - faded splendour of the Somoza era when the islands were a popular resort - lit up the runway. In between, stalls were set up, selling sweet plantain, sweet potato, fish and pork, cooked on the recycled hub of a car wheel, flames flickering in the dark. Coconut cakes are the greatest delicacy.

Nora stayed as a guest of an important Creole family of the Atlantic side - the Hookers. Miriam Hooker had been first press secretary at the Nicaraguan Embassy in Washington until May 22nd that year, when she and a colleague, William Vigil, a political counsellor, had been ordered by the Reagan administration to leave the country. This was supposedly in retaliation for something which had happened in Managua. Four US diplomats had been caught out in espionage operations. The diplomats had left Nicaragua after this discovery, although they had not been required by the Nicaraguan government to do so. Miriam believes her deportation had a lot more to do with her style of publicity work - which involved direct contact with members of the ordinary people in the States rather than sticking to press releases through normal channels. (7)

Both Miriam and her brother Ray were strong FSLN supporters. Ray had been kidnapped by Contras while campaigning for the FSLN slate during the 1984 elections; he was released a month later. After the Sandinista success at the polls he was co-opted, along with Hazel Lau and Luis Carrión, on to the national commission to draft the statute on Atlantic Coast autonomy. Miriam went down to the Embassy in Zimbabwe after this.(8)

Nora also met up with her old friend Lea Guido, who had herself just been diagnosed with cancer. Lea remembers, 'I was really depressed. She took me to the doctor, she looked after me although she was ill herself.' (9)

When Nora got back to New York, Miguel d'Escoto took her to his old medical friend, Kevin Cahill, who has his practice on Fifth Avenue. 'The surgery in Cuba hadn't really worked out,' says Dr Cahill, 'and she was in a bit of a mess - on top of having simultaneously to take up her duties at the United Nations.' Dr Cahill took over responsibility for Nora's condition and it was he who supervised her hospital stays from then on - and they were numerous. But this was also the start of a personal friendship as Nora would spend time at the Cahills' home and Kate (Kathryn) Cahill, a writer and photographer, sometimes travelled with Nora when she went on speaking tours. (10)

Over the summer of 1986 there was a period of particularly intense lobbying. This was a crucial time for Nicaragua: the United States House of Representatives was debating another military aid bill for the Contra. They had already rejected two packages that Spring and the Nicaraguans were still hopeful that US public opinion against Vietnamisation in Central America would influence the vote again.

However, Congress finally passed a $100 million budget for the Contras, to be handed out over the next nine months. In addition, it was agreed that the CIA were allowed to carry out covert activity in the region (although US personnel would not be permitted to give training or assistance to the Contras within 20 miles of the Nicaraguan border).

In fact, the CIA had also planned a $400 million 'capital investment programme to provide covert logistical support, training, communications and intelligence' and make available to the Contras material purchased from CIA funds, although such material would technically continue to be CIA property. A process was to be established by the House of Representatives 'to monitor both the probity of the Contra leadership and the prospects for peace.' (11)

'This is a declaration of war by the United States against Nicaragua,' was Daniel Ortega's statement the following day. 'The new situation will require more stringent enforcement of the October 1985 state of emergency

153

proclamation. We have applied this so far with excessive flexibility but from now on political attitudes favourable to the Contras and Mr Reagan will no longer be tolerated. He who loves Nicaragua, the country and the people, let him stay in Nicaragua and he who loves Reagan, let him go to Miami or to the mountains with the counter-revolutionaries.' (12)

The FSLN National Directorate closed down *La Prensa*, arguing that, in a state of war, censorship was necessary to preserve national security. This closure created a scandal in the US media who conveniently failed to mention both the fact of US censorship of Nicaraguan affairs and US funding sources for Nicaraguan media. The newspaper remained closed for over a year. In addition, some of the pro-Contra clergy (who also supported anti-Sandinista radio and magazine outlets in Nicaragua) were expelled.

There was serious talk of invasion by the United States at this point. The forthcoming 19th of July celebrations was an obvious target. 'If the Yankees think they'll win by invading Managua, they'll soon find they're wrong,' said a university colleague of mine, Marissa, at this time. 'There's a safety net around the capital. But more than that, we've decentralised sufficiently for each region to operate independently, to carry on fighting. Anyway, the people are forewarned. Our defences will be mobilised all over the country.'

Nicaragua still had a lot of support. The Contadora Group had already expressed their displeasure at the US decision. Bernardo Sepúlveda, Foreign Minister of Mexico said, 'It is regrettable that some countries use instruments of war in the name of peace.' (13)

Ironically, the next day the International Court of Justice made its second ruling against the United States. They found that the United States was under an obligation 'to make reparations to Nicaragua for damages caused by its illegal intervention' and that 'it should cease and refrain from such acts immediately.' They found that the United States had violated international law on four main counts, including the training and financing of the Contra. (14)

Miguel d'Escoto announced the news from the Hague over the radio: 'It has been a victory for peace... It has been a triumph for all the people of Nicaragua, for all those who accompanied us in the Way of the Cross for Peace and Life. That sacrifice was a clamour not ignored by God.' (15)

Nora may still have been asking herself questions about her faith in God. But if this was a Phyrric victory, she made the best of it. She immediately composed a letter to the President of the Security Council: 'I have the honour to request you to convene an emergency meeting to consider the escalation of the United States Government's policy of aggression against Nicaragua, which threatens international peace and security.' (16)

Nora's first meeting in the Security Council was on July 1st 1986. But Miguel d'Escoto - who came up to New York to put the case for Nicaragua - made the speech that day. Nora's task was to lobby as many countries as possible and persuade them to ask for an invitation to participate in the discussions. Andrés Aguilar, ambassador for Venezuela (which had a seat on the Security Council at that time), spoke in support of Nicaragua, arguing that aid to the Contra violated international law and the principle of non-intervention - principles to which all subscribed there in the United Nations - and that this decision seriously jeopardised relations between the US and Latin America. (17)

The US reply to widespread criticism was that firstly, Congress did not approve a military aid package to the Contra as such, that this was only part of a package of economic aid to the Central American countries of Guatemala, El Salvador, Honduras and Costa Rica and so should be considered in its wider context. And secondly, as regards the International Court, its judgement only demonstrated what the United States had being saying all along, that 'the Court was simply not equipped to deal with a case of this nature involving complex facts and intelligence information... '

The Council met again the following day, when Mr Ghebo of Ghana, Chair of the Group of African States at the United Nations, spoke in support of Nicaragua, likening the Contras (supported by the United States)

155

to the terrorists in Angola, supported by South Africa. Ten other countries supported Nicaragua and the World Court ruling; only El Salvador spoke in favour of the US position. Nora made a short speech in which she focused on the use of the international forums for resolving disputes: 'We are a country who respects the law and we brought our case to the International Court... The United States, on the other hand, becomes the accuser, the judge and the executioner and attempts to do justice, according to its own interpretation, against our country.' (18).

On July 3rd, the day before the American Day of Independence, the Afghanistan delegation (who had asked to attend discussions) referred to the United States as 'morally bankrupt', saying, 'We strongly believe the United States administration has betrayed the letter and spirit of the United States Declaration of Independence.' (18)

Within the United Nations Nora was held in high regard, usually known simply as 'Norita'. She made herself felt right from the start. It is true that part of her impact was due to 'her condition of woman in a massively masculine world. Apart from her, only two or three out of 159 countries have sent women representatives to the greatest world organisation,' as Real de Azua put it. But beyond that, it was because she demonstrated herself 'with an extraordinary capacity for work and a fine psychological perception, naturally elegant, cultured... committed to compensating for the meagre diplomatic resources of her country with a frenetic activity, although always hiding the inevitable fatigue,' remembers one of the UN reporters, who admired Nora. (20)

Elaine Sciolino, the chief of the *New York Times* United Nations bureau, was rather less generous in her appraisal of Nora's effect: 'With high cheek bones and 5 feet 11 inches in the high heels she insists on wearing, she cannot help but stand out. Her movements, in fact, are so carefully watched that during a recent Security Council debate, a woman diplomat said, "the moment Nora Astorga crossed her legs, all the eyes in the room were off the speaker and on her."'' (21)

It took Nora a little time to get used to handling herself under pressure at the United Nations where Sciolino described her, 'chain-smoking Marlboros and fingering her jewellery'. Nora herself recalled her lack of confidence in the public forum: 'My first speech in the Security Council I found very difficult.' After all her experience, she still claimed that 'speaking in public has never been one of my strengths. I've now learned how to do it, but I know I will never be a great orator. I've learned to convey what I want to convey and to speak in a coherent form, to say things correctly, without slipping into the vernacular. Learning public speaking has taken its toll; to read a speech is easy but to improvise there in the United Nations... it's not easy.'

Nora's modesty about her own skills is reflected in what other people have to say about her. For example, Carlos Tünnermann said, 'She attained real stature because of her style of diplomatic intervention, she was a noble figure, always negotiating for peace and understanding. Yes, she was known for her rhetoric, her attack skills, but always using words characterised by morality and maturity.'

One reporter describes Nora as follows: 'Avoiding the (typical) burning ideological declamations, favouring a pragmatic approach, playing the diplomatic game to the full without ever relinquishing her defence of the Sandinista cause, she did more than most to improve the image of a Nicaragua often perceived as excessive and chaotic, seeking alliances in the East.' (22)

'Even those who criticise her politics acknowledge that Astorga is a skilful diplomat.' Elaine Sciolino noted.

Mary Anne Weaver of *The Christian Science Monitor* suggests that Nora, during a short visit she made back in Managua that August, was specifically primed to win over conservative US congressmen by Daniel Ortega - following the rather unexpected advice he had received from the anti-communist representative of California, Congressman Robert Dornan, at a party held by the Reverend Jesse Jackson. 'An improbable undertaking?' asks Weaver. 'Hardly... For Nora Astorga has rarely

157

undertaken much that seemed probable and there is no indication that she is about to change her ways.' (24)

Tensions

Nora's job at the United Nations was certainly not an easy one. Her US counterpart was General Vernon (Dick) Walters. He was a highly decorated army man, with much experience in Latin American affairs. He served in Vietnam, for which he was awarded the Croix de Guerre and was Deputy Director of the CIA between 1972 and 1976. He must therefore have had a great deal to do with Somoza and his henchmen. He had acted as special advisor to Haig on Latin American affairs, making several unpublicised visits to the region. (1)

It was Walters' job to block Nicaraguan diplomatic manoeuvres. But the 'usually formidable general', as Mary Anne Weaver describes him, suffered formidable setbacks when Nora squared up to him. Apparently, during the Security Council session on 2nd July 1986, much to the delight of other delegates, she, eyeing him directly across the table, waited until Walters had finished a somewhat disjointed address and said very calmly, 'He's lying.'(2)

In the Security Council Walters tended to make personalised attacks on other representatives and slurs on those delegations who supported Nicaragua. When the Security Council met again at the end of July, at Nora's request, to discuss the situation between Nicaragua and the United States for the twelfth time, he even managed to sneer at the level of support that Nora had brought into the Council chamber, 'I do not believe there will be any problem with applause at the end of *my* statement. *I* have not packed the gallery.' (3)

Walter's speech on this occasion reflects that complete inversion of reality that characterised the US position throughout its ideological conflict with the Sandinista government. 'The United States yields to no nation in its commitment to international law. No member of the United Nations has a stronger or longer record of respect and support for the peaceful resolution of disputes in accord with the UN Charter... Nicaragua is a country which has sought to overthrow the governments of its neighbours and to deny its own people the right to self-determination.' (4)

This level of distortion of reality was closely linked with US control of media coverage of Nicaraguan affairs. The CIA's disinformation programme, which paid local journalists throughout Central America to generate anti-Nicaragua, pro-Contra press stories and financed fake press releases by Contra officials, not only side-tracked journalists from following up real events, but also had a blowback effect on legitimate news reporting in the United States. As one researcher points out, 'The CIA fabricated material became part of the information picked up by the Agency itself and by other US government bodies, notably the State Department, which in turn used this information to formulate foreign policy in the Central American region.' (5)

Walters gave a lengthy diatribe against the sins of the Sandinista government, which included a reference to 'the thousands of political prisoners' - whom Nora had tried, although Walters did not mention this. After criticising the Sandinistas for not fulfilling its promise of political non-alignment, he went on to refer to the support of the Non-Aligned Movement for the Nicaraguan position as 'astonishing and disturbing.' (6).

Nora's response was short and simple. 'Nicaragua is ready to work for peace... Even now the United States has the chance to amend the situation... It can still abide by the ruling of the International Court by immediately ceasing all military and paramilitary activities in and against Nicaragua. *We are here. We are ready to find that solution and understanding.*' (7)

'We've had so many tense moments that I find it hard to say which was the most extreme,' said Nora, thinking of these battles with Walters. Absolute conviction of her cause was what sustained her: 'I always believe that we have the advantage because of our political, moral and legal base, but that doesn't make my fear disappear.'

But Nora was also a soldier and had been decorated herself. Moreover, whatever she may say about her hidden fears, her negotiating

160

style was deliberate and effective. In the Security Council, she adopted a respectful and somewhat innocent tone which inspired one of her friends there to observe that she was the Little Red Riding Hood of international diplomacy (presumably playing to the United States' Big Bad Wolf). She enjoyed the joke immensely. (8) And she also admitted: 'The United Nations is a negotiating forum *per se* and that interested me a great deal.'

As in every other stage of her life, Nora threw herself into her new rôle completely. 'She never screwed up her face at combat in the mountain or in the city, in uniform or in civilian clothing, before the press or before the world in the protocol and formality of high diplomacy,' writes Sofía Montenegro, using the guerrilla metaphor for Nora's work in the United Nations. 'She ambushed so many Yankee politicians with her intelligence, disarmed manoeuvres with her bravery and audaciously mounted operations in alleyways and corridors, she persuaded ambassadors and nations, weaving third world alliances against dispossession, illegality and injustice, conspiring with whoever she could against the war.'(9)

Nora's skills were also useful during Daniel Ortega's visits to the United States. When he came up to New York to speak to the Security Council meeting at the end of July, she helped draft his speech 'which was more conciliatory in language than any he had made from the same podium', according to Elaine Sciolino's article. She also doubled as tour agent and accompanied Daniel and Rosario Murillo on a street campaign through New York - the Brooklyn waterfront, the Riverside Church, housing projects and newspaper editorial offices.

Within a few months Nora had established herself in New York. 'Serving as Nicaragua's only direct contact to much of the world, Astorga will become the focal point of the upcoming General Assembly session on Central America, aiming to win broad support for the Sandinista revolution and discredit American policy in the region.' (10) Nora was also elected Chair of the UN Group of Latin American and Caribbean States for this 41st session.

161

She had experienced a major disappointment when, despite her intense campaigning, the Non-Aligned Movement voted against the bid to have Nicaragua host the movement's Eighth Summit conference in the summer of 1986. The chair falls to the leader of the host country and would have guaranteed high visibility for Daniel Ortega. The conference was held instead in Zimbabwe. However, Nora succeeded in ensuring that 15% of the discussion in Harare was focused on Nicaragua, Contadora and the Central American peace process, with several condemnations of US intervention. And she continued to lobby for Nicaragua as the site of the next summit conference in 1989. (11)

Nora became known for 'her fierce logical argument and her highly feminine style,' writes Jennifer Uglow, who also records that Nora had a habit of sending a red rose along with her diplomatic memos. (12). A colleague of Nora's at the Nicaraguan Mission explains that, in fact, Nora kept a note of the birthday of all the Ambassadors in the UN and made sure her office sent each a card and a rose on that day. (13) Victor Hugo Tinoco did not know about this, but, shrugging his shoulders, he obviously felt it was completely in character. 'That was the way she was. She might send flowers, why not?'

Nora was a regular visitor to the delegates' lounge, kissing and shaking hands with colleagues as she entered. This is the lounge which Sciolino describes as 'a kind of male club where horse-trading is conducted over cigars and scotch' and which Jeane Kirkpatrick herself, when US delegate to the United Nations, characterised as full of more 'rank sexism than any other arena I have ever been in my life.'

In such ways, Nora was able to transform her previous image as the Mata Hari of the revolution, her notoriety as the seducer and possible assassin of the CIA collaborator General Pérez, into yet one more ingredient of an extraordinary personality. 'She wears her past like other women wear perfume,' Sciolino reported one delegate as observing.

162

Nora became particularly friendly with representatives from the Latin American States, for example, Bernado Sepúlveda of Mexico, André Aguilar of Venezuela and Luis Gonzalez Posada of Peru, all countries which were involved in the Central American Peace process. She was also popular with her African colleagues, since she continued to be involved in the fight against apartheid, and in return received much support for the Nicaraguan cause. Nora actually did quite a lot of travelling in Africa - Kenya in 1985, Zimbabwe in 1986 - and she especially enjoyed a visit to Ghana as the guest of her colleagues in the Security Council (Ghana was also an elected member). As an active participant in the Non-Aligned Movement, she had many allies and was remembered as 'a good friend' to both the (then) USSR and the Arab group. (14)

Nora not only cultivated fellow ambassadors but also their wives, with whom she met regularly. (15). She even managed to maintain cordial relations with her enemies outside the United Nations chambers. She attended receptions at the United States mission and spoke 'important nonsense' to her main adversary, General Walters, who later commented on the courage it required of her to attend (16).

'My personal relationship with Vernon Walters has been normal. I would say at a purely personal level I have not lived with the US-Nicaraguan tension always upon me. The war of aggression has not been translated into aggressiveness toward me by the North American representatives,' she recalled.

Nora also began studying the history of the United States, trying to get a grip on the reality of a society which is bent on 'keeping people in the dark or making certain that people don't get interested in the reality of what happens outside their own little world... I'm trying to understand the dynamic of that society which is so very different from our own... so that I can get a better picture, a better understanding of who the people are and what is going on there.'

Nora was tirelessly public, despite her illness. 'She was much invited, to churches, to universities, to feminist associations; she was a member of the War Affairs Council which has branches in all the main cities and involves different organisations. From San Francisco to Chicago she had a very high level of activity. After her mastectomy she never really recovered, but she worked with the same enthusiasm, she accepted all the invitations. We used to swap invites - if I couldn't go, she would go instead,' recalls Carlos Tünnermann.

She enjoyed a great deal of public prestige both because of her personal charm and because of her work in diplomatic intervention. Because she spoke good English, she was able to converse without an interpreter and have direct contact with US counterparts and citizens.

She had serious admirers, too, Victor Hugo Tinoco remembers: 'Bernstein (the composer) was madly in love with her, he used to send her flowers; we first met him in London - where Miguel's brother Francisco, was Nicaraguan ambassador - on our way to Washington.' Bernstein was also a friend of Kevin and Kate Cahill.

On top of all this activity, Nora sought advice on novels to read or plays to see. Victor Hugo, who was Nora's interlocutor in Managua while she was at the United Nations, would come up to New York with the delegation for the UN General Assemby every year in September. He would stay in Nora's house and they would go out together, taking advantage of all the facilities of New York. 'She didn't talk about her illness, I just kept her company, we wanted to enjoy ourselves...'

All in all, this is the picture of a woman who wanted to live life to the full, a woman with a sense of humour - one of the key features which allowed her to commit herself without falling into sectarianism and to maintain an avid curiosity about the world and its people. (17)

Throughout all this period of intense activity, Doña Muriel was there for Nora, with her all the time, providing the support she needed. 'I don't know why she never spoke about that publicly,' reflects Guadelupe Salinas.

'Doña Muriel was Nora's substitute with the children, Nora couldn't have done what she did without her mother. And her mother had great vitality. You could see the continuation of that vitality in Nora. Maybe that was why Nora never really recognised the value of what her mother did for her, they were too alike...'

There's a different picture we can paint of Nora, coming home exhausted - partly from the illness, partly from hard work; depressed or angry, because of each new obstacle put in her path by the United States; worried or nervous about a forthcoming speech she had to make. She would try to maintain good spirits with visiting friends and with her children, but in fact she probably spent little time at home. 'She never let me see how much she suffered. Nobody knew. But New York was bad for her nerves. It was hard for me to see her going out all the time, so elegant,' remembers Doña Muriel.

Nora didn't know how much longer she would be a voice out there, in the world forum, representing Nicaragua not just before the United Nations but before 'a whole load of countries.' It must have been this that gave her an edge, made things clearer, everything more urgent and immediate. Moreover, despite her extraordinary success as a diplomat, Nora did admit that 'it has been very hard for me to adapt myself to the task of being a diplomatic representative in the United States.' Despite her natural elegance and flamboyant style, she didn't like the protocol of 'having to dress every day in coat and tie.' She once told Daniel Ortega that 'my work wouldn't be so difficult if I could wear blue jeans at the United Nations. But I most certainly cannot!' 'Diplomacy would be different if we could dress as we please, wouldn't it?' she muses to her interviewers from *Envio*.

She was still playing a rôle - however much commitment she brought to the part and however much she might lose herself in it - in a man's world. There's an implication that even at home in New York she couldn't relax entirely, as she says: 'Every time I get back to Nicaragua I put on my jeans and sit out in my patio.' It was only among her own people that 'she could speak freely without weighing every word.'(18)

165

A poem written by Safiya Henderson Holms, after observing Nora at a party ('she came to all the parties'), captures something of the tight coiled spring that was Nora's life in New York:

> she sat on the edge
> much of the time
> waiting, watching, ready...
>
> with hawk's eyes proudly
> watching the room...

A Nicaraguan came to sit near her with his guitar and began to play some of the old favourites and, as he played,

> then nora folded quietly
> like flowers do for night
> and brave woman warrior
> nora was a child again...
>
> and nora could sigh (19)

Throughout autumn and winter 1986, Nora worked under extraordinary pressure. Her strategy at this time was to request special meetings of the Security Council or the inclusion of special items in the plenary sessions of the General Assembly, calling on the United States to comply with the ruling of the International Court of Justice to cease aggression against Nicaragua. This was against the backdrop of US aid to the Contra and a build-up of military strength along the Honduran-Nicaraguan border. Nora had plenty of experience in public speaking during this time.

General Walters' strategy was to veto the motion before the Security Council a second time. But even the United States has no power of veto in the United Nations General Assembly. Here Nicaragua gained a significant success: 3rd November 1986 was the first time in the history of the United

Nations that the Assembly condemned a country for not respecting a sentence of the International Court of Justice. (20)

Three more resolutions were passed; the first condemning the use of mercenaries in Central America (November 5th); the second, after a long and polemical debate, requiring all states to respect the principles of international law (18th November) and the third, on November 21st, deploring the continuation of the trade embargo against Nicaragua (in contravention of a previous UN resolution) which was carried by 86 votes to one. Vernon Walters got up abruptly near the end of the debate and left the hall. The US strategy was not to vote at all. (21)

At another emergency meeting of the Security Council, in December 1986, Nora asked for support against attacks on civilian and military targets in Nicaragua by fighter planes from Honduras. She pointed out the Honduran government had repeatedly refused Nicaragua's proposal to send an independent commission under the supervision of the United Nations to investigate the situation at the border. Why, if the Honduran army were not guilty of armed aggression against Nicaragua, was Honduras not prepared to accept observers? (22)

Nora was back on national television and in the morning newspapers over relations with Honduras. While she claimed that the Honduran attack had been carried out 'on orders from Washington,' General Vernon Walters argued this was in retaliation for the Nicaraguan army crossing the border. Senator Richard Lugar, appearing on CBS News with Nora, suggested that the Nicaraguans had made a pre-emptive strike because the Contras 'have a fairly good training situation now. The arms and supplies will be coming into them.' Nora retorted that, 'No money can make a difference... The Contras do not have any political-social base.'(23)

United States persistence in its actions was highlighted by two cases which, though highly publicised, seemed to make no difference. The first involved Eugene Hasenfus, the US Marine captured by the Sandinista army when they shot down a C-123K cargo plane overflying Nicaragua. He was carrying arms for the Contras. Miguel d'Escoto flew up to New York with some of the documents that had been found in the plane. On 10th October he spoke to the United Nations General Assembly. 'We hold you responsible,' he said, calling on President Reagan and Secretary Schultz, 'and some day you will have to give an accounting before the Lord - for all the bloodshed and suffering inflicted on so many innocent people by your insatiable desire for domination.' (24)

The facts are made clear in the issues of *Envio* for November and December 1986 and February 1987. On 11th October Hasenfus was interviewed by Mike Wallace on CBS *Sixty Minutes*, admitting that he was employed by the CIA. On October 16th Congress gave final ratification to the $100 million aid to the Contra and the policy of putting the CIA in charge of the war. Senator Tom Hawkin's proposal to investigate the Hasenfus case was defeated. It was clear the CIA had been operating outside the law and Congress had decided they had no moral authority to criticise them.

Next, the discovery that high-up White House officials had been selling arms to the Iranian government caused a major scandal to break at the beginning of November. It was discovered that part of the money obtained from the sale of arms to Iran had been diverted to the Contras. While this link was being investigated in the US courts, special envoys Elliott Abrams and Philip Habib were visiting selected countries in South and Central America, spreading the word that, 'There is no longer room for a neutral attitude towards Nicaragua. Taking a middle ground is tantamount to approval of communist acts.'

Nicaragua did not leave herself unprotected. On 8th November the people commemorated the 25th anniversary of the founding of the FSLN and the 10th anniversary of the death in combat of Carlos Fonseca. A quarter of a million people stood under the noonday sun listening to the long speeches and watching the military parade. For more than 90 minutes some eight thousand soldiers filed past, followed by tanks, anti-aircraft rockets and modern radar. Helicopters - MI-8s and MI-24s - flew overhead. 'We have heard the message,' said the US State Department.

Nicaragua's allies continued to speak out against the United States in different forums. For example, at a meeting of the Organisation of American States General Assembly in Guatemala City, 'How is it?', asked Luis Gonzalez Posada, the Peruvian Ambassador, 'that a member of the OAS can legally approve the financing, training and arming of an irregular army to attack another member state of the same organisation?'(24)

The OAS, jointly with the United Nations, published a communiqué offering a range of services to help relieve tensions in Central America and in support of the Contadora effort, including the monitoring of the border areas and dismantling military bases.

On December 18th the Foreign Ministers of the Contadora and Lima Groups called for an end to US aid to the Contras and pledged to renew their efforts to achieve a negotiated peace in Central America. They planned a tour through the region early in the new year. This tour was sabotaged to a large extent through intense diplomatic pressure. Vernon Walters criticised the decision of the Brazilian Secretary-General of the OAS to take part in the tour. The conflict in Central America is merely regional,' he argued, 'and ought to remain so. I'd therefore like to bring into question the legal basis for the participation in the tour of Baena Soares... And I'd like to repeat my request for a detailed explanation of the purpose of this tour,' he said ingenuously. 'We don't want the OAS to be converted into the caboose on a train, when we don't know where the train is going...' (25)

Pérez de Cuéllar of Peru, the UN Secretary General, who was to take part in the tour, was also subject to questioning. Never one for great subtlety, the United States added 'gunboat diplomacy'. They sent battleships, including the Iowa (known as 'the messenger of death' because it is equipped with nuclear rockets) 'to demonstrate US interests in the region' and positioned them off the Nicaraguan coasts. Then began the large scale US military manoeuvres in Honduras (only 20 kilometres from the Nicaraguan border) and in Panama on the Costa Rican border.

'Neither Contadora nor the United Nations nor the Organisation of American States can do very much if there isn't the political will or the sincerity to find peaceful solutions or the desire to sacrifice positions,' said Cuéllar later in Mexico (26).

After Contadora's departure from Costa Rica, President Arias demanded the 'democratisation' of Nicaragua as a condition for peace. El Salvador, Honduras and even Guatemala followed this lead. The 'San José Peace Plan' was suddenly born. Costa Rica became the official standard bearer of US policy in the region and Contadora lost her birthright.

Nora attended the third conference of Contadora and Central American countries with member nations of the European Communities which was held in Guatemala City at the beginning of February. It ended with a joint declaration of support for the Contadora principles of non-intervention and diplomacy as the only means through which a peaceful solution could be reached.

She also took part in an extraordinary meeting of the Bureau of Co-ordination of the Non-Aligned Countries of Latin America and the Caribbean, in Georgetown Guyana, the following month.

But after that it was the San José Peace Plan (which had originally been cooked up between Reagan and Arias over the Christmas period and garnished by Madrigal, Habib and Abrams) now called the Arias plan, that took centre stage. Of course, Arias had become increasingly hostile since Nicaragua had begun to highlight Costa Rican complicity in the war and had tarnished their liberal international image. The Costa Rican initiative was designed to remove Contadora from the negotiating scene or at least to reduce her to a mere symbol. (27)

In the event, Daniel Ortega quickly saw much in the Arias plan worthy of study and agreed to go to the next Esquipulas meeting. The plan, which included a clear prohibition of aid to the Contras, was supported by US Congress in March and endorsed by Contadora itself in April. (28)

Despite the disappointments involved in this series of manoeuvres, Nora recalls the positive aspects of her work at the United Nations, in particular 'the opportunity to learn deeply about other realities. Especially the realities of the Third World, because, independent of the differences we may have among ourselves, we are all poor countries, we have all been exploited, we have all suffered intervention. Because of this there is solidarity, there is greater understanding... I am witness to the solidarity Nicaragua has in all the international forums... There are countries that don't have anything specific to do with us, but who see us as a small country under attack and one that has principled policies; because of this they feel they should support us... For many countries of the Third World, we represent the possibility of finding a new way to overcome the problems of poverty.'

The Struggle Continues

In 1987 Nora missed the International Women's Day celebrations in Nicaragua for the first and last time since the Triumph.

Rousing speeches proclaimed that, 'The FSLN must lead the struggle for awareness-raising and the education of the entire society towards the eradication of discrimination against women, which obstructs their full incorporation into the revolutionary process... in its belief that Nicaraguan women will continue devoting their best efforts and energies to the defence and consolidation of this revolutionary process, which has created and guarantees the conditions for the full realisation of their human potential.'(1)

However, Nora continued to be involved in promoting women in her work at the United Nations and through this, she had a lot of contact with the women's solidarity movement in the United States. Many US citizens were sympathetic to the Nicaraguan cause. For example, MADRE was a new women's organisation set up in 1984 to stop US intervention in Nicaragua 'by developing a true exchange between people here and people there: mother to mother, woman to woman.' (2) MADRE was (and still is) sponsored by women writers, politicians and performers, including prominent African Americans like Alice Walker and Jacqueline Jackson. But its strength comes from the links made between women at the grassroots, exchanging letters, fund raising in order to send material aid and campaigning to highlight the worst effects of US aggression on women and children. All over the United States, women's groups continued throughout the 1980s to organise events and exchanges in support of Nicaragua. And Nicaraguan women continued to provide a special rôle model for their North American sisters who were inspired and moved by the strength, the accomplishment of these women.

MADRE had the status of a non-governmental organisation (NGO)at the United Nations, providing briefings and a woman's perspective for the Commission for Human Rights as well as for UNICEF and a range of consultative committees. As a very new organisation, they had a lot to learn about the best way to operate. In an interview in New York on 24th September 1996, Vivian Stromberg, now Director of MADRE, reflected on Nora's influence: 'Nora understood the importance of playing a rôle in the international arena, we learnt a lot from her about working with groups that we did not exactly see eye to eye with, what gains could result from those kinds of relationships, the formalities of life at the United Nations. She was a very important person to us - and she came to every party.'

Like Nora, MADRE didn't work within a narrow definition of women's issues, but attempted to provide a woman's viewpoint to everything that was happening in the world, everything that was relevant to women's lives.

'Nora was fiercely passionate about the emancipation of the Nicaraguan people, about her work and mostly about children. This was why her struggle was such an inspiration to women in the United States and why she continues to be a great inspiration today. She was really driven by a commitment to improve the world for the next generation. She's an important rôle model for me, for example,' said Vivian Stromberg, 'I was moved by a woman who saw the interconnectedness of all aspects of her life and who lived by a set of principles that I admire, a commitment that I resonated with - and I think that's true for a lot of people. The very very sad thing is that her story, along with so many other stories of women who pave the way for us, gets lost - so that younger people don't get enough nourishment from that. We need to know where we came from, we didn't invent practically anything ourselves, we've only built on what's happened before us - and we need to do a better job of carrying that history, passing it along, not repeating it but learning from it... Nora stood up to the United States, that's no small thing, that means a lot to a lot of people in the world, not only here but in other countries where people are struggling for the integrity of their nation, of their person. I believe Nora's story would add light years to people's lives if they could know it.'

Nora developed personal friendships with a number of US women with histories of supporting Nicaragua, including Kathy Engel, the poet and then Director of MADRE, Susan Meiselas the photographer and Eleanore Kennedy the lawyer whose husband and partner had provided legal advice for Nora. However, as Susan Meiselas says, 'I think we both would have liked to have had more time with each other. Our lives were too pressurised with the events of that period.' (3)

Nora also had contact with Nicaraguan women based in the United States and working in solidarity through the *Casa Nicaragua* network. This was a system of houses or clubs which were set up across the US in the early 1980s by the FSLN, to give information about Nicaragua, its life and culture. They hosted visitors from Nicaragua, organised events, provided an informational resource about the revolution - newspaper cuttings, videos - which were used in schools. They organised brigades to visit and work in Nicaragua and were a contact point for Nicaraguans living in the United States. Arcadia Brenes of the New York *Casa Nicaragua* recalls Nora's visits: ' She was compassionate and modest, so easy to talk to.' (4)

Many US citizens working in solidarity met Nora through the *Casa Nicaragua* or through the sister-city programme. In a speaking tour in autumn 1986, Nora travelled across the United States to nurture these twinning projects, from Portland Oregon (twinned with the Port of Corinto) to Concord New Hampshire. According to Don Casey of Agendas International, many organisations would ring Nora directly at the Nicaraguan mission at the United Nations to request a visit: 'she had her own relationships with support groups and arranged her own outreach work.' (5).

Agendas International was based at that time in the same building, but their relationship was much more with Carlos Tünnermann at the Nicaraguan Embassy in Washington and their involvement with the Peace Process, as regards direct dealings between the US government and Nicaragua. They were heavily involved in Daniel Ortega's regular visits to the States in this connection, in negotiations with Contadora, and Esquipulas. 'The United Nations was not our main concern, since this involved multi-lateral intergovernmental lobbying.' In addition, the United Nations is not part of US territory, it stands on neutral ground with its own laws and postal system, 'it doesn't get a high profile here,' added Casey.

Therefore, a lot of Nora's work was 'invisible' in the United States, both her formal diplomatic work and the informal liaison work she did with solidarity groups. It wasn't reported in the US media. However, in April 1987 Nora was invited to speak to the American Society of Newspaper Editors, on the subject of 'Peace in Central America: The Next Step.' This was a very prestigious gathering and Don Casey encouraged her to take up this formal speaking engagement. ('Because of her illness we normally didn't push her to accept these invitations as much as we might have done.') He worked with her on the speech and accompanied her to San Francisco.

As Andrew Viglucci introduced her, he spoke about Pedro Joaquín Chamorro, editor of *La Prensa*, whose assassination influenced Nora's decision to become involved in military action in 1978. Chamorro 'was known by many in this room' and three months before his assassination was awarded the annual María Moores Cabot award from Colombia University for a distinguished contribution to bettering American understanding. What concerned those present was that *La Prensa* had now been closed down by 'that left-wing dictator, Daniel Ortega.'

This occasion is published on audio-tape and it provides a valuable example of how Nora operated in public representation of her country. She never raises her voice - in fact her intonation does not vary much at all - but her speech is clear, fluent and confident, with an accent more reminiscent of the Creole English of the Afro-Caribbean people of the Atlantic Coast of Nicaragua than of the United States.

On the tape you can hear her swallowing from time to time, a telling indication of the tension and effort that is involved. Nevertheless, she states her position with precision and passion. At one point she says: 'We don't ask you to love us. The only thing Nicaragua is asking for is respect. And for you to leave us in peace.' Her intonation rises here and she repeats the phrase in the same way. 'Leave us in peace'.

Criticisms were often made against Nora that she was 'just a pretty face, a resonance box and what is put into it is decided in Managua.' (6). As the media succeeds in distorting reality, the personal and the political are confused, with prejudices against a country reflected in images of the person who represents it, and vice versa. Nora was constantly in a position where she had to defend both herself and Nicaragua at the same time.

Dora Zeledón observes dryly, that 'logically, if you represent your country, you support the official position, you don't give your own opinion. It was Nora's personal qualities, her competence, her charm and audacity, that meant she could carry out that rôle most effectively.'

In this defence rôle, Nora used a certain irony, a certain defiance or bravura, which often amounted to an offensive. For example, at the meeting of ASNE which Nora addressed, the editor of the *Miami News* attempted to characterise the repressive nature of Nicaraguan press censorship by quoting an anecdote: the match results of an 'exiled' Nicaraguan boxer, Alexis Aguello (then living in the United States) had been cut from *La Prensa* one morning. After assuring the questioner that the match had in fact been televised on (state controlled) Nicaraguan television, Nora continued dryly: 'Of course we feel flattered when everything Nicaragua does is put under the magnifying glass, but we'd like to tell the United States - do your share, too! Stop the war.'

Don Casey refutes the suggestion that Nora ever had any real difficulty answering hostile questions. He quotes this event with the editors as evidence: 'she dominated that.' He also refutes that Nora was 'overprogrammed' by the FSLN leaders. 'You only had to meet Nora to know that she was entirely her own person.'

Kevin Cahill remembers his wife accompanying Nora on a college trip to North Carolina, where she had to face some aggressive questioning.

176

Nora had her own way of deflecting this aggression. 'You probably think of Nicaragua as a banana republic, well just remember that, like bananas, we may be small but we're very sweet.' (7)

'We don't actually believe that socialism is a contagious disease, ' she told students at New York University on another occasion. (8)

Kate Cahill recalls Nora looking up with a shy smile of surprise when she was greeted with enthusiastic applause by yet another group of US citizens at the University of Virginia, only four months before she died. Not knowing beforehand whether they would be friends or foes, she had no set speech. 'Her message was the truth and she delivered it with pride and dignity, believing that no amount of dressing it up or down could alter the facts.' (10)

When Nora was criticised for leading an extravagant lifestyle in New York while people in Nicaragua were facing a deepening economic crisis, she retorted, according to Elaine Sciolinos' article: 'You can't expect me to wear blue jeans in the Security Council.' In fact, the amount of money the Nicaraguan mission spent on diplomatic representation was relatively small (US$1500 per month) and no-one in the United States knew that the rest of Nora's expenditure (her house, her family and so on) was paid for out of her mother's diminishing capital.

'She never took a cent,' is how people talk about Nora's financial outlook. 'She never asked for a car. (She used an old blue Mercedes). She paid everything for herself,' said Consuelo Romero. Furthermore, Nora's family had lost most of their wealth under the 1985 Property Act.

Nora's irony and defiance was coupled with a continuing modesty: 'she would never boast about anything she'd done,' says her mother. The combination is reflected in the way Nora spoke about herself, as if she stepped back and watched the part she was playing, with some amusement and wonder - yet always prepared to defend it.

Even when Nora was working at the United Nations, it is difficult to find any mention of her in the Nicaraguan newspapers. Was this deliberate on her part? By the middle of 1987 she, and many with her, knew that her illness had made her life a race against the calendar. 'Eternal accomplice of the people, she suffered her secret, together with thousands of others, so as not to call attention to herself,' was how the journalist Sofia Montenegro explained it in her obituary for Nora.

However, in June 1987 Nora was awarded the highest tribute by the government, the Order of Carlos Fonseca. And there is one small mention of her in *Barricada*. When she returned to Nicaragua for a holiday and to take part in the 19th July celebrations, she was involved in a training seminar organised by Foreign Minister, Miguel d'Escoto for diplomats working overseas: *en la trinchera internacional, aqui no se rinde nadie!* (in the international trench, no-one surrenders!) She was among the group that flew to the Atlantic Coast to visit Yulo, the centre of the peace negotiations over there, along with Victor Hugo Tinoco and Daniel Ortega, Carlos Tünnermann and Cesar Arostegui, Ambassador to India. Yulo is a small town situated on the river Huahua, inland from Puerta Cabezas.

'The visit was special firstly because *compañera* Nora Astorga was presented with their pictures of peace by Miskito children... It was a moment completely charged with emotion,' Arostegui recalled. (11)

Luis Carrión presided over a commemorative ceremony in Juigalpa to celebrate the town's liberation in 1979... Daniel talks about 'a great carnival of happiness' and Victor Hugo remembered the joy of the insurrection, when the Guard surrendered eight years before... Daniel would have liked to be a writer, a poet. The Order of Carlos Fonseca was awarded to Oliver Tambo on July 19th, but there is nothing about Nora... (12) However, she went up to Estelí to the celebrations with Doña Muriel to receive her award, 'of course, she was so proud,' said her mother.

These few weeks were the last that Nora would spend in Nicaragua in comparative health. She wanted to enjoy them, not to talk about her illness.

The chemotherapy was taking its toll, she was losing her hair, she was losing weight, she looked weak. But she never gave in. For her, 'The real Nicaraguan woman is not the one who wants to cry in the face of tragedy.'

Daisy Zamora describes her 'trying to get rid of death with a gesture, as if shooing away a fly'... carrying on as if she didn't see the unequivocal signs, deliberately ignoring the knowledge, talking of superficial and frivolous matters. Her face is a mask, made up to cover death, rouge frozen on her cheeks, flashes of blue and gold eye shadow, burgundy wine moistening her lips. Daisy likens Nora to a canvas, retouched to hide the cracks in the paint that is flaking off. 'You play the game deeply and all of us politely follow your lead - with tense complicity - our sight blurred by your fateful splendour.' (13)

Looking back on Nora's life, what would she change, if she could, if it meant she could go on living? Daisy wanted to know and yet 'I daren't ask you anything (since you behave) as if you had no worries or regrets.' Nora was as defiant as James Dean, she wrote, in her suit studded with stars, full of metal zips 'your body still rebelling, even in its shroud, denying death.'

Researchers from *Envio* made an appointment to have an interview with her, 'not needing to explain the timing nor what we would do with it later... There was not a single allusion to (the fact that she was conscious of nearing the end of her story) although it was implicit in the reason for the interview.' (14) For Nora it was a chance to take final stock of her life. 'It's always good to look back, to see where you've come from,' she told them. She reconstructed her autobiography 'without hurry, with a clear intent to be open and with pleasure, laughing often...'

She did allude to difficulties at one point, but immediately dismissed them: 'When I get weary or impatient, I think of all those who have died, I think of the mothers who have their children mobilised in the army... I have no right to be weary... After all I have been privileged. I was born where I was born, in this unique country. I met people who helped me grow. I had the opportunity of participating in the struggle against the dictator and now in reconstruction and the creation of a new society. What more could I ask?'

It seems she was a woman who had no regrets, despite heartaches along the way. 'The revolution filled Nora,' explains Guadelupe Salinas, 'it was enough for her... she rose above everything else.' Carlos Tünnermann agreed. 'She was inspired, utterly convinced that her fight was just, that she had to fulfil her responsibility to the very end.'

The regrets were about things she hadn't had time to do yet. Nora told *Envio* that she, too, would have liked time to write, about various subjects, including her ideas about women: 'Our centuries long history, a millennia of exploitation, during which we've carried an image of ourselves that isn't real. Even now, we educate our daughters differently from the way we educate our sons. But it is we who have had to take responsibility for our children's lives and that's why it was us, that's how it was with women that we really made the revolution... But there is never time (to write down my ideas). We are always in such a tense situation because of the war that the only thing you can do is to try to figure out how to keep going forward and hope that later... but now there doesn't seem to be time for anything else,' she commented poignantly. '

On returning to New York, Nora had to prepare for her rôle as Deputy President of the 42nd General Assembly of the United Nations, where she continued to fight 'in the trenches' against the United States, those other 'machos.' As Sofía Montenegro describes Nora, 'She was already dying when she drove back General Vernon Walters with her well-shot arguments: "Has someone given the United States the right to award patents in the matter of democracy? Who has given the United States the right to commit aggression? one illegal act after another? to use the name of God in vain and bring death and destruction for those of us who wish to live in peace?" She vented her anger on her enemy with her calm face and

180

pale beauty, a monument to Nicaraguan dignity, although she was wounded to death.'

Perhaps, Sofía concludes in her obituary, it was this combination that made Nora so invincible. 'it was always difficult to imagine so much firmness beneath her sweetness, so much transforming passion alongside her serenity, so much energy under her gentle nostalgic look.'

More than anything, though, it was Nora's stoicism in her illness that enabled her to carry on at this stage, that 'supermachismo' which had filled Chester with awe in guerrilla days. 'They (the National Directorate) used her right up to the end,' claims Doña Muriel, while conceding that 'they also gave her the chance to be useful right up to the end.' For it would have been even harder for Nora to sit and do nothing, waiting for death.

Nora maintained her commitment to the struggle for freedom and justice in Southern Africa, which 'is the struggle of the international community.' The previous year she had spoken out in the General Assembly on apartheid, when she quoted Nelson Mandela. 'The ideal of a free and democratic society where all persons will live together in harmony and with equal opportunities...(this) is an ideal for which I hope to live, but if necessary, it is an ideal for which I am ready to die.'(15)

In the 42nd Session Nora was a member of the UN Council for Namibia and spoke on the situation in Angola and Namibia in the Security Council. South Africa itself did not recognise the Council which had been set up administer the pending independence of Namibia in 1967. And, despite years of discussion, international sanctions had still not been applied to South Africa by the UN Security Council 'because of the continued misuse of the veto power by two of its permanent members.' These were the United Kingdom and the United States. (16) The US, of course, was still applying sanctions to Nicaragua. As Nora pointed out, 'the hypocrisy of (Reagan's) actions and the deceitfulness of his arguments become clearer each day. When sanctions serve his interests, he applies them enthusiastically. When they affect his interests, sanctions automatically become illegal.' (17)

Nora was honoured during her lifetime in the United States. For example she received a special award (for Law in the Service of Human Needs) from the Law School at Queen's College (City University of New York) for her 'contribution to the advancement of international law and diplomacy.'

Victor Hugo Tinoco accompanied Nora to see the musical Cats at the Winter Garden on Broadway at this time. Elaine Paige was playing Grizabella, the Glamour Cat who haunts the streets at midnight in the tattered rags of former finery and sings about her memories of the old days in the sun ('I was beautiful then'). Now the withered leaves collect at her feet and the wind begins to moan. 'I must wait for the sunrise / I must think of a new life / And I mustn't give in.' Along with the sad lyrics and the haunting melody of 'Memory', this song finishes on a poignantly courageous note: 'If you touch me you'll understand what happiness is. Look, a new day has begun.' (18) 'I remember, that brought the tears to her eyes,' says Victor Hugo.

Another old friend was with Nora for the 42nd session. This was Grethel Vargas, also a former student of Colegio Teresiano, who had been Chief of Staff at the Ministry for Foreign Affairs. 'In 1986 she proposed my name and in 1987 I joined her as First Secretary to the Mission. She always promoted women. She would push you to think "Can I do that job?" and she put on a lot of pressure, saying " I need you here to help me."'

Grethel Vargas describes the first time she spoke in the General Assembly - a daunting prospect. 'The US Ambassador made a statement against the Sandinistas and I asked for the right to reply. Nora came when I asked her, after the initial debate, and she helped me with the reply, she showed me how to be careful, not to use rhetoric, to use real arguments and support every point. She was sitting at the back but I asked her to leave before I made my reply, I was too nervous. But that was how she encouraged me. She taught us all how to be proper diplomats and we learnt another lesson from her, that the essence of politics and diplomacy is humanity and dignity.' (19)

Grethel Vargas is still at the United Nations mission: she has modelled herself on Nora to some extent, with short black hair, a smart dark suit, gracious and generous with her time and information. Despite changes in government, it is still the same people there who worked with Nora, a professional diplomatic corps.

Rita Clarke, Miguel d'Escoto's sister, was working at the Nicaraguan Embassy in Washington at this time. She remembers that Nora also encouraged her secretary at the United Nations, Norma, to study law, and she sent others to study languages. 'She recognised talent, she gave a lot of women opportunities,' says Rita, highlighting this as a key factor in Nora's greatness. (20)

Comments such as those quoted in Mary Anne Weaver's article the year before, that Nora surrounded herself 'with a largely inept staff' and that 'she runs the mission rather like you would run a Marxist guerrilla camp' (whatever that implies) (21), have to be seen within this context - the work involved not only in developing an effective diplomatic front with a small pool of inexperienced people to draw from, but also in ensuring that women were well represented in this front.

Nora was having to take more time off work for chemotherapy. But she would be back next day, speaking in the General Assembly, supporting her staff, carrying on as if nothing had happened. There was just one day that Grethel remembers when Nora came into the mission very depressed, the day she had to buy a wig. It was hard for her, losing her hair.

But Nora's passion for life and her will to live transcended this. As well as defending her nation's children against insuperable odds in the United Nations, one of those women 'who have always stepped into the fire when there is no other way to save a child', she was 'a mother who gave her children in her free time the full warmth of her heart.' (22).

In addition, the mission staff were a team, her extended family and were invited by Nora to share all the important (North American) celebrations, Halloween, Thanksgiving, Christmas. Nora loved to arrange big parties for all the mission's children. 'My daughter was just seven, then,' remembers Grethel Vargas, 'All the children went to Nora's house.' In ways like this Nora tried to protect her own children from the possible psychological effects they might suffer from living in the country of the aggressor. (23)

Confrontation with the United States was intense that year. But, despite everything, this was a period of optimism. The third draft of the Arias Peace Plan had finally been signed in August. This included cease fire agreements, an end to states of emergency, an end to aid from governments to all irregular or insurrectional forces in the region.

Nicaragua at least carried out their part of the agreement. The National Reconciliation Committee was set up under the leadership of Obando Y Bravo. A unilateral cease fire was called by the Sandinista government. *Radio Católica* and *La Prensa* were allowed to resume production. Not only that, but the Law of Autonomy for the Atlantic Coast was passed in September.

However, while the United States had outmanoeuvred themselves on the diplomatic front, they had finally succeeded in making the Nicaraguan economy scream. The costs of fighting the war against the Contra, the cut-off of US economic assistance and the reduction and eventual cut-off of US trade meant that Nicaragua was finding survival increasingly difficult. Since the virtual military defeat of the Contras, the Eastern bloc countries were less inclined to subsidise the Nicaraguan economy, given their own problems at the time. Trade agreements with neighbouring countries such as Venezuela and Mexico were increasingly difficult, not only because of Nicaragua's lack of foreign exchange, but also because of the pressure put

184

on those countries by the United States. Analysts of this time commented that, by any known laws of economics, Nicaragua should have gone under long before this. (24)

The Final Exile

In the autumn of 1987 Nora began to weaken rapidly. There had been a plan in gestation for quite some time, among Nora's North American friends - including the photographer Susan Meiselas - to make a documentary film of Nora's life, 'to put the record straight.' But the project was destined to come to nothing. 'At first Nora was not willing to acknowledge that she was going to die and in order to approach the film properly, that was necessary. Then there was time spent in securing financing for the film, which Michael Kennedy finally managed to do. But Nora was too sick by then to do the film,' explains Susan Meiselas. (1)

Nora called Carlos Tünnermann, saying that she wanted to spend a few days in Washington and went to stay at his house with her mother and her children. She visited art galleries, there was a favourite painting she remembered in the Phillips Gallery, by Renoir... Carlos took her to see the River Potomac, the famous basilica at the Catholic University, to Georgetown. She wanted to revisit the days of her youth.

Nora had to spend more time in hospital. On the 22nd December she told her mother: 'I don't know how much longer I have left.' And for the first time, she communicated to her mother that she was afraid of dying without absolution.

Although she had long claimed not to be a practising Catholic, Nora had attended various church services while in the United States. The eulogy she gave at the funeral service for a Dominican sister, who had been active in Nicaragua, moved the congregation of St Vincent Ferrer Church (in Manhattan) to tears. She had received communion in summer 1996 when she took part in the 25th anniversary celebration of Miguel d'Escoto's ordination as a priest in Ossining, NY.

But it was not Father Miguel who helped her at this point. Nora asked to see a US priest, Father José Hann, a patient in the same hospital who was also suffering from cancer. She said that it was he who helped her to finally accept her illness, to come back to God, according to a former teacher of Nora's. After she had spoken to him she felt prepared for death, for the fact that it was God's wish. Afterwards, Nora became calm again, said her mother. The event also affected Father Hann. 'He came out crying with emotion at her tranquillity, her resolve, her lack of fear of death', Miguel d'Escoto remembered. (2)

Despite this emotional and physical upheaval Nora was there at the United Nations on 23rd December to sign the International Sugar Treaty.

Nora told friends that she wanted three things before she died - to visit Ghana again, to go ice skating, and to return to Nicaragua. She did go ice skating with her children that week. Kathy Engel, Nora's friend from MADRE, uses this as a metaphor for the way Nora lived her life, as this extract from her poem shows:

> you are skating
> negotiating on ice
> writing speeches with your
> skate blades
> eating mangoes with your
> mittens
> breathing circles of frosty air...

The poem also expresses the solidarity of friends and admirers with Nora in her final battle:

> and those who love you
> everywhere
> known and unknown...
> find little ponds and indoor
> rinks
> and huge lakes
> and even rivers that stand still
> for a moment

187

and skate
skate furiously with you. (3)

Nora spent Christmas 1987 with her family and friends. There was a big party at her house, as usual, for everyone from the mission, when they exchanged presents and took photographs. Nora told them: 'I want you all to be together,' Grethel Vargas remembers. On 26th December she took her youngest children, Alberto, Ricardo and Norita, for a trip to Bear Mountain. Then she presented herself at the hospital again for an operation on the womb. But the operation couldn't be carried out; the cancer had spread to her lungs. She knew there was nothing to be done.

Grethel Vargas was there with Nora's deputy, Julio Icaza. Nora was in an oxygen tent, but she said: 'Let's have a glass of margarita' (this was her favourite drink). She sent Julio to fetch a bottle and he smuggled it back in under his coat, along with some crystal glasses.

Nora's close friends Michael and Eleanore Kennedy were also with her. On New Year's Eve they called Carlos Tünnermann and Rosita Pereira, who flew to New York. Carlos recalls: 'She was there surrounded by her friends and her children. She said, "I want to die in Nicaragua but they won't let me travel. I'm not well enough to travel. And it's too expensive to send a hospital plane." In the end, Michael Kennedy said, "Don't worry, Nora. I'll pay for the plane." But the only one they could arrange at the time was a US military hospital plane. And the irony was that they had to clear the flight with the State Department - who had to clear the flight with the Contra. Since Nora was in an oxygen mask and could barely breathe, the plane had to fly very low over Nicaragua, lower than 6000 feet. (4)

Nora continued to joke, said Grethel. 'If I'm travelling in a Yankee plane, you'd better get a message to Humberto in Managua, tell him not to shoot me down by mistake.' (Humberto Ortega was head of the Sandinista Armed Forces). 'We all drank champagne with her to say goodbye,' remembers Carlos Tünnermann.' That was the last time I saw her.'

Dr Kevin Cahill, along with the Kennedys, accompanied Nora down to Nicaragua. 'It was a sign of her courage and femininity that, half an hour out from Managua, as we were crossing Nicaragua from the Atlantic towards the Pacific, she wanted to be made up. When we arrived at Sandino Airport, she walked down the steps and got into the car on her own. Then she collapsed.' (5)

Nora's arrival in Nicaragua was like a 'great transfusion of health and happiness. She met up with her friends, went to the beach, ate in the markets,' recalls Miguel d'Escoto. (6) She even turned up at the Foreign Ministry, asking Miguel to put her to work. She still had a great presence, a great spirit.

Nora's mother remembers another, elderly doctor, coming down from the United States to visit. 'I must know Nicaragua,' he said to Nora, 'if all Nicaraguans are like you.' She took him to visit the tiny islands in lake Cocibolca, just out from the city of Granada.

Rosita Pereira returned to Managua at the end of January and visited Nora at home. Like everyone who visited her, she was struck by Nora's continuing vitality. Another friend commented, 'She opened the door herself, I was shocked, I'd heard she was dying, but there she was talking generalities, not about death, but affectionately about past times... In fact, of course, she had to make a big effort not to fall...'

Nora was always more concerned about other people despite the gravity of her illness. Jorgé Jenkins, her first husband, came to visit and they talked. Jorgé had been Ambassador to Brazil and had remarried, to a friend of Nora's. After he left, Nora said to another friend: 'He's changed a lot, his wife has helped him to mature.' She was happy about this, very positive.

Nora was particularly concerned about her children, that they stay all together as a family, with her mother, not only her own children but her nieces (Lidia Ruby's children) too. 'She was sure about her mother, who had helped her all her life... It was a mutual support - her mother had confidence in Nora, too, for Nora had always helped her,' said a former teacher of Nora's.(7) Her children, of course, were very affected by her illness, especially Muriel, who had lost her mother once before - when she had disappeared after Operation *El Perro*. Now she was going away again, for good. The strong one was Dafne, who took after her mother both in appearance and in temperament, very calm, very determined.

Nora never lost her smile, her hope of life. 'I went to visit her two weeks before she died. She was wearing a headscarf to cover the hair-loss, the traces of her illness were really visible then. She wanted to go to the sea, she said, to listen to the murmurs of the waves, they calmed her,' remembers Dora Zeledón.

Nora also made her peace with Chester, who was still in Costa Rica. She rang him from her Managua home and at first he was bitter with her: "You stopped me speaking to the children," he accused her. "I know, I was a fanatic," she agreed. "But I see things differently now, I see things calmly." 'We talked for two or three hours like that. The following week I heard she was dead.'

A few days before she died, Nora was moved to the Military Hospital in central Managua. There she received valuable support from a former teacher, a nun from the Colegio Teresiano, who gave her communion several times. 'She'd had a blood transfusion, but, when I went in, I saw Rosario Murillo was with her, they were talking about their old schooldays and singing the special hymn to Santa Teresa - Teresa had always been Nora's favourite as a young girl, her rôle model, they had the same style, both very dynamic.'

This friend also testifies to the calmness with which Nora approached the end. 'She put the revolution to one side, she talked about her illness, about her death, she had to reconcile herself to that... but she died in peace. Her life had been of such service.'

One day Nora called and said with her characteristic understatement: 'I'm not feeling so good.' Her friend arranged for a priest to come to her then, Padre José Manuel Guijo.

190

In the interview with *Envio* several months previously, Nora had mentioned her special fondness for the nuns and her desire to make her peace with them. Guadelupe Salinas felt this part of the interview had been edited in some way by the Jesuits, that religion was never much of an issue with Nora. However, Sister Rina Molina said, 'I know Nora was very close to this teacher when she died and that her presence was very significant to Nora and especially to her mother.' (8)

Close friends like Lea Guido and Guadelupe Romero were with Nora at the end. And Guadelupe Salinas said, 'I believe she had a serenity at the end, a satisfaction in having done what she had done.' 'Who knows if she reconciled herself with God?' asks Sister Rina Molina. 'Who are we to judge what she did? The important thing is that she fought for justice, that was what she believed in ...'

In January the Verification Commission set up by Esquipulas had called for the cut-off of aid to the Contras as an indispensable requirement for peace. In the United States the progress of the Arias Plan and the indignation of millions of ordinary North Americans combined at the same moment.

On February 2nd 1988, MADRE organised a vigil on the steps of the Capital, joining the veterans and ex-CIA employees who had been fasting there. It was reported in the Spring issue of *MADRE Speaks*: 'We wanted to make a very clear statement about the effect of Contra aid on children both in Nicaragua and the United States.' They held up photographs of children wounded in Contra attacks before Christmas on Bonanza, Siuna and Rosita. 'This morning in New York City, more than 12,000 children woke up in welfare hotels and thousands more were shivering on the streets... Our children are dying of neglect while we send millions of dollars to the Contras who are killing Nicaraguan children,' explained one of the speakers at the vigil. (9)

On February 3rd the House of Representatives voted to deny the administration's request for military aid to the Contras. The Contras, beaten in both Congress and the field, embraced the Arias plan. (10) 'When she died, there was the possibility of a peace agreement, she did have some hope... but we all knew that, even if a cease-fire agreement were signed, it would be difficult to carry out the process of reconciliation with the Contras, it would take a good time...' said Victor Hugo Tinoco.

Meanwhile there was a national day of political mobilisation in Nicaragua, called by Bayardo Arce, who spoke to a thousand newly recruited volunteer reserve soldiers in Masaya, part of a campaign to hasten the demise of the Contra forces. On the front page of *Barricada* was also reported the death of nine children, all younger than thirteen, from Contra attacks in Quilalí and Wiwilí. (11)

That was the day that Nora died, on the 14th February 1988. It was appropriate, felt Miguel d'Escoto, for her to die on the day of lovers, 'because she was a person overflowing with love, love of life and love of the people, at whose side she had always fought.' (12) Daniel Ortega announced she would be awarded the funeral honours of Heroine of the Fatherland (sic) and of the Revolution.

Her death was overshadowed, however, by the announcement of monetary reforms a few hours later and it was this story that led on the front page of *Barricada* the following day, with a picture of Daniel. The reforms, in the hope of stabilising the economy and increasing production, included a new currency, salary readjustments, new prices and a new rate of exchange. Apparently sixty thousand people had known about the coming changes but had kept them secret - Nicaragua went into the Guinness Book of Records! (13)

'It was such a pity, there were so few people at Nora's vigil that night, because everyone was counting money,' remembers Gloria Tünnermann who went with her aunt Rosita Pereira to the vigil at the family house in Colonia Becklin. 'Rosario Murillo was there, redecorating the altar, she was bringing plants in from outside and putting them all around the casket, then she sprinkled flowers over the floor...' (14) Lea Guido had prepared Nora's body, dressed her and made up her face.

On 15th February Nora arrived at the Foreign Ministry, as she had done so many times before, entered through the same door, this time in her coffin carried on the shoulders of Sandinista soldiers. She had come home to say goodbye. The occasion was reported in *Barricada* the following day. The coffin was hidden beneath a multitude of flowers, and a large photograph of Nora, as a younger woman, with a wide laughing smile, bright eyes and thick long hair, was positioned on top of the wreaths.

The National Directorate of the FSLN, members of the General Assembly, ministers and civil servants, ambassadors of allied nations, formed the guard of honour in the slow march past, to take their leave of her, one by one. All her colleagues at the Foreign Ministry gave her their usual respectful and affectionate greeting ('la Norita').

The first tribute was made by Lea Guido: 'She was beautiful, inside and out.' Walter Ferrety, who had been involved in Operation *El Perro* called her, 'A worthy representative of Nicaraguan woman.' Xavier Chamorro, Pedro Chamorro's brother and editor of *El Nuevo Diario*, described her death as, 'A loss for the diplomatic front and for the Revolution.' Miguel d'Escoto referred to her as, 'A daughter, a sister and a wonderful comrade in arms.'

The funeral was held at Government House and celebrated by ten priests. Father Alvaro Arguello, referring to the Christian tradition of burying the dead, likened Nora to a fertile seed which had borne, and would continue to bear, fruit. Carlos Mejía Godoy's Peasant Mass was sung, testifying to the love of the land, the unity of the people and their commitment to fight for their country - a fitting farewell for Nora:

> A thousand peasants
> sing to you together.
> We come from the hills
> with our knapsacks

packed with love,
because you are the Mighty One,
the Judge, the Counsellor,
you are the Champion
of all my people.

> *(Meditation)*

The fishes in the water
want to come with us
and leap up excited,
gleaming and delighted
with heart-flung fellow feeling.

> *(Communion)*

Let us join our hands to be
linked once again
in love, today for Nicaragua,
in one huge chain.
Let us join our hands to build
a mighty wall
to defend all our people
forever as one.

> *(Farewell Song)* (15)

Nora was buried in the Eastern Cemetery in a plain white tomb encircled
with a low white fence with simple flowers wrought in it. On the gate is
the inscription:

> Nora Astorga Gadea
> heroine of the nation
> guerrillera
> ambassador of peace,
> love and life
> 9 Dec 1948 - 14 February 1988

Daniel Ortega spoke a final farewell at the graveside: 'We must fill the void she has left with the power of her example. Nora, Hero of the Nation and of the Revolution.' (16) Then, as *Barricada* describes it, 'with deep solemnity and amidst the tears and choking of those comrades in arms who had accompanied the funeral march, the coffin containing the body of Norita, the Sandinista heroine, was let down into the earth.' (17) And so Nora passed into the collective consciousness, the common history of the people of Nicaragua which sustains the future, a heroine who is always present. As she herself put it, 'The dead are part of us, they are our living force, those who accompany us and help us.' Maybe it was this belief that helped Nora reconcile herself to death.

'Nora didn't die,' Grethel Vargas said later, 'she's just there with the vanguard, the *comandantes*, Carlos (Fonseca), German (Pomares), José Benito (Escobar), at the side of Oscar Turcios and Gaspar García Laviana (Martin), who took her by the hand and said: "it was a hard task but you carried it out."' (18)

Gioconda Belli dedicated the novel *La Mujer Habitada* which she published later that year 'to Nora Astorga, who will keep on being born.'

Amongst the mausoleums (Nora's grave is flanked by the much more imposing family Wheelock and the Gutierrez vaults) Doña Muriel and Nora's children received the condolences of Daniel Ortega and Sergio Ramírez.

Even then there were tensions between Church and State. All the sisters from the Colegio Teresiano attended Nora's funeral 'and the family was very grateful,' emphasises Sister Rina Molina. 'It was actually unusual having nuns attend a funeral under the Sandinista government! and I remember afterwards a reporter questioned the right of the sisters to be there! He demanded to know: what was the relationship between the nuns and Nora?'

A mass was held later for Nora at the Colegio Teresiano, which Doña Muriel attended.

In the US media, a considerable amount of space was dedicated to covering Nora's death. The United Nations flew its flag at half mast and paid homage to her. A book of condolences was opened at the Nicaraguan seat and signed by leaders of the other UN delegations. 'In reality, representatives of all continents and political tendencies, international officers, official journalists, everyone recalled with emotion and sadness the figure of Astorga, or simply Nora, whose passage through the United Nations will not be forgotten quickly,' wrote one UN reporter. (19)

Even General Walters, as acting president of the Security Council, expressed his grief at Nora's death, at the opening of the session where they were to discuss the South Korean air crash: 'I am sure I speak for all members of the Council in saying that we shall miss her greatly.' (20) The Secretary General Javier Pérez de Cuellar, who was on a tour of Africa, sent a message of condolence to Daniel Ortega. Hugh Scotland wrote a poem in Nora's honour:

> May Nora Astorga's life be immortalised, as history bears testimony
> To one of God's rare gifts to patria, and to the nation among many
> Upon whom light will always shine and blessings be bestowed,
> To a sacrifical life lived, achievements and faith restored. (21)

On 23rd February, a mass was held in New York at Saint Patrick's Cathedral, a Memorial Service organised by Friends of Nora Astorga. It was attended by more than eight hundred people. 'The place was packed,' remembers Don Casey of Agendas International. 'They carried her picture down the aisle.' It was full of celebrities and diplomats. Many people spoke. The actress Susan Sarandon recalled her first meeting with Nora, when, as a member of the first MADRE delegation to Nicaragua, she had attended the International Women's Day celebrations in Managua in 1984. 'For me she defined dignity personified and integrity, possessing qualities one rarely finds in leaders.'

'The mass was even reported in *The New York Times*, and it was not usual for them to report that sort of event,' observes Carlos Tünnermann.

Representatives from 50 United Nations missions were present and those from Peru and Argentina also spoke. The United States was not represented. Many friends from MADRE were at the mass. MADRE had run a large In Memorium notice in *The New York Times*, advertising the service and including an unattributed poem, which highlights the symbolic importance of Nora's life:

> we see you
> and we see a woman;
> we see a country:
> young and beautiful and determined to live. (22)

But Nora had provided her own epitaph:

'The people are my constant source of inspiration... I believe there exists today no other reality like ours, no other reality in which, even with such serious limitations, each of us feels we have an obligation to society and tries to fulfil it with imagination and a sense of humour... the spirit of struggle that our people share, that generosity, has given me pride in being Nicaraguan.'

Epilogue

The Nicaraguan economy was crippled. Monetarist measures had been imposed, cutting public expenditure, sacking public employees, lifting price controls. There was devaluation, hyperinflation and a drop in the social wage. Finally the United States succeeded. The Nicaraguan economy screamed. And there was a change among the people. Everyone looked so tired, they almost looked hard.

The United States continued to intervene in Nicaraguan affairs. In October 1989 they voted US$9 million to support the election campaign of the United Nicaraguan Opposition and in the general elections on February 25th 1990 the Sandinistas lost to the UNO coalition. Violeta Chamorro became the new President. Since then the Nicaraguan people have lived under a right-wing government and the economic situation has worsened for the poor majority. An estimated 44% of the population are now living in 'acute poverty' as defined by the United Nations and many of these households are headed by women - who continue to try, by whatever means, to provide for their children's future.

After the obituaries, the interview that Nora had given to *Envio* the previous year was published in various forms, in English by *Envio* in Nicaragua, in Spanish by CIPAF (*Centro de Investigación Para la Acción Feminina*) in the Dominican Republic, in German by the journal *Das Argument*. On the 29th February, the United Nations General Assembly paid homage to Nora Astorga with speeches from the Heads of each of the regions; the documentation of this runs to nearly thirty pages. (1).

On March 3rd 1988 Grethel Vargas and her female colleagues at the Nicaraguan Mission in New York sent a fax in Nora's honour to Daisy Moncada in Managua to be read out at the International Women's Day celebrations in the Foreign Ministry. It read, 'Norita, in this field of international politics where women fight to occupy the place they deserve, you elevated the rôle of the Nicaraguan woman: we want to tell you that we won't mourn you, we will only imitate you.' (2)

MADRE ran a tribute of several pages of poems and photographs in their Spring 1988 newsletter. Apart from these and the biographical notes produced by the newly-named Nora Astorga Women's Information Centre at AMNLAE, I have not found anything written about Nora since her death.

Nora received posthumous awards, such as the *Testimonio de Roque Dalton* from Mexico, in May 1988, which still hangs in her mother's bedroom. That year MADRE dedicated their new conference room to Nora, their new video and their First National Gathering. Events in Nicaragua, particularly related to law, were named in her honour, for example 'The First Nora Astorga Seminar on Women and Legislation' organised by the Women's Secretariat of the professional association CONAPRO - itself named after the 'Heroes and Martyrs' of the revolution. Kevin Cahill dedicated his collection of essays to 'Miguel and Norita who kept faith with the poor and the oppressed.' (3)

The painter Guillén produced several large canvases, lifelike portraits of Nora based on press photographs from her diplomacy days, which reflect her combination of confidence and serenity - rather than her mischievous side; one canvas hangs in the AMNLAE reception area, another dominates Doña Muriel's sitting room.

Nora's family received no financial help. Doña Muriel tried to keep everyone together, as was Nora's wish on her deathbed, but things have been very difficult for her, particularly as she gets older. She couldn't afford to send the girls to the Colegio Teresiano.

Finally she had to let Alberto Secundo and Norita go to live with their father, José María Alvarado (Chester), who is back in Managua running a seafood export business. Children and father have managed to

199

restore their relationship despite the fact that Alberto once believed Chester was an evil person.

Dafne now lives with her father, Jorgé Jenkins, and is in Costa Rica studying. Muriel stays with her grandmother but won't speak about her mother - the suffering was too great. Alberto, Nora's first free child of the new Nicaragua, for whom she fought on the Southern Front, was also very attached to Nora and has had a lot of problems adjusting since her death

Doña Muriel carries on her struggle to keep the family going in the face of all the difficulties. When I arrived to visit for the second time, I was given a message by Norita José that read, 'I couldn't wait for you because of a family emergency...'

What would Nora be doing now? I asked Victor Hugo Tinoco. He replied, 'She would still be in there, fighting. She wouldn't have given up, or turned to individualism.' Consuelo Romero goes further: 'If she were still here, the country wouldn't be in the situation it's in. She would be leading the Women's Commission...'

But Nora lives on as an important symbol for other Nicaraguan women, in what has become one of the most interesting women's movements in Central America. According to Lea Guido, who now works with the Pan-American Health Organisation, 'Nora influenced the present profile of women, because of her life, her autonomy and determination, the fact that she managed to get respect from men, to compete with them at work and to fight for the same rights as men, to work towards a new form of relationship between men and women... this is a message for other women.'(4)

Through espousing different images of herself, Nora transcended simple definitions of who she was and achieved a level of integration that few women have attained. As Sofía Montenegro said in her obituary, Nora has given us an alternative model of womanhood to aspire to, a new and multi-faceted identity.

More than anything, for me, Nora represents the inspiration that drives a woman to fulfil her professional potential and to perform in public life, despite the fact that this hardest of all challenges continued to take its toll. Nora chose to defend her children's future in the public arena rather than stay at home to protect them: we need to recognise that this is a painful choice and one that takes courage to pursue.

Moreover, she consistently used her position to further the opportunities of other women who worked around her, through mentoring, training and nominating them for promotion. Uncovering this 'invisible' work she did on behalf of women helped me to balance the fact that Nora never publicly spoke about the women in her life: the bond with her sister, the love of her daughters, the limitless support she counted on from her mother despite their differing political viewpoints, the co-counselling she had with her best friend. It seems unlikely that she took these for granted. Rather they were the continuum that helped her to keep on fighting.

Notes

Prologue

1. Recitations, songs and verses from Que Causa Tanta Alegría? *Barricada* Managua December 4th 1994: 1C-4C

A Good Catholic Girl

1. Margaret Randall 1981:118
2. Rosario Murillo interviewed by Marc Cooper Nicaragua's new first lady *The Houston Post* January 6th 1985:1-2
3. Vidaluz Menesis in Randall 1994:149
4. María Cristina Najlis interviewed by Margaret Nixon in Managua, July 31st 1996
5. Sofía Montenegro in her obituary of Nora *Barricada* February 16th 1988
6. Daisy Zamora Afeites de la Muerte in 'La Mujer Nicaragüense en la Poesía':346. The poem was written for Nora and describes her on her visit to Nicaragua in July 1987, some months before she died. The title means 'The Make-up of Death'
7. Leaflet from the Museo Nacional de Nicaragua, Museo Sitio Huellas de Acahualinca 1994
8. Daisy Zamora Radio Sandino in 'La Mujer Nicaragüense en la Poesía':378
9. Joaquín Cuadra interviewed in Randall 1983:138-9
10. María Cristina Najlis interviewed by Margaret Nixon in Managua, July 31st 1996
11. Statutes of the FSLN: Statement of Purpose in Tomás Borge 1992:248
12. ibid.
13. Nora Astorga interviewed by Art Harris *The Washington Post* October 4th 1984: Style B1

Rebellion

1. Anibal García UCA, Managua 1986
2. María Hartmann interviewed in Randall 1983:152. María Hartmann was a North American nun who came to work in the poor neighbourhoods of Managua.

3. Conchita Alday was the warname of Sandino's wife, Blanca Arauz.

4. Keesings:21953

5. ibid.

6. *kupia kumi* is Miskito - one of the indigenous Indian languages of Nicaragua, still spoken on the Atlantic Coast.

7. Daisy Zamora 1992:35

8. Joaquín Cuadra interviewed in Randall 1983:140

9. Nora Astorga interviewed by Art Harris The Sandinistas' Sister-in-Arms: The Ardor of a Revolutionary *The Washington Post* October 4th 1984: B1

10. Keesings: 22933A

11. 'Our Lady of Guadelupe' was first seen in 1531. The Indians of New Mexico believed that their goddess Tonantzin had returned to them in the person of Mary.

12. Dr Carlos Tünnermann interviewed in Managua December 5th 1994

13. Interview by Elaine Sciolino *The New York Times Magazine* September 28th 1986:28-29

14. Catholic University of America Yearbook 1968

15. Interview with Art Harris, op. cit.

16. Interviewed in Randall 1981:119

Forward with the Front

1. Jorgé Jenkins Moliéri, August 25th 1996

2. Interview in Randall 1981:119

3. Milú Vargas interviewed in Randall 1994:129

4. Randall 1981:119

5. 'El Pequeño Ejercito Loco' deals with the Mexican-Nicaraguan operation and was published in 1959 by Editorial Triangulo, in a print run of 5000, along with two other books about Sandino. The following year La Imprenta Nacional de Cuba took on the three books and printed 20,000 copies of each, which were sold at 35 centavos a book.

6. Randall, op. cit.

7. Daisy Zamora Radio Sandino in 'La Mujer Nicaragüense en la Poesía':374

8. See Leonel Rugama <u>The houses remained full of smoke</u> in Livingstone 1993:56-59

9. Randall 1994:21

10. Omar Cabezas' 'La montana es algo más que una inmensa estepa verde' (published in English as 'Fire On the Mountain') tells the story of life in the *guerrilla*

11. Randall 1981:119

12. Gioconda Belli in Randall 1984. Reproduced in *Envio* Vol. 7 No. 83 May 1988:32

13. Jorgé Jenkins Molieri, August 1996

14. Randall 1981:119

15. María Hartmann interviewed in Randall 1983:162

16. Nora Astorga interviewed by Art Harris, op.cit.

17. María Hartmann, op.cit.

18. Randall 1981:119

19. ibid.

20. According to the article by Elaine Sciolino *The New York Times* September 28th 1986

Separation

1. In Randall 1983:160

2. Gioconda Belli <u>Managua</u> in Zamora 1992:295

3. *The Times* Washington correspondent January 27th 1972:1

4. Timothy O'Leary *The Times* January 28th 1972:1

5. *The Times* January 28th 1972:4

6. In Randall 1983:162

7. Interviewed by Marc Cooper *The Houston Post* January 6th 1985

8. Interview by Art Harris *The Washington Post* October 4th 1984

9. In Randall 1981:119

10. Interview by Art Harris, op.cit.

11. In Randall 1994:174

12. Randall 1981:120

14. 'La Mujer Habitada':171

15.These and the following comments come from Nora's interview with Randall 1981:119-20

16. ibid.

17. Tomás Borge 'The Patient Impatience' 1992:447

18. ibid:445

19. Quoted in *Barricada* February 16th 1988

20. Lea Guido interviewed by Dierdre Hyde and Margaret Nixon in San José July 17th 1996

21. Randall 'Sandino's Daughters Revisited' 1994:16

22. In Randall 1994:131

23. In Randall 1981:4

24.Primera Asamblea de AMPRONAC *La Prensa* September 30th 1977

25. Lea Guido interviewed in Randall 1981:16

26. In Randall 1981:127

27. See Collinson (ed) 1990:140

28. In Randall 1981:127

29.*Envio* Women and Revolution in Nicaragua Vol 6 No 78 December 1987:19

International Women's Day

1.Margaret Yayko in her Introduction to: Tomás Borge La mujer y la revolución Nicaragüense 1983:4

2. Jenny Pearce 'Under the Eagle' 1982:46

3. See Rius 1982: 110-11

4. Nora's account and comments on the *El Perro* operation appear in Randall's 'Sandino's Daughters' of 1981

5. Chronology in Livingstone 1993:252-53

6. Nora and the Dog *Time Magazine* April 2nd 1984:24

7. En Washington: Que se vaya Somoza *La Prensa* January 14th 1978:1

8. *La Prensa* January 12th 1978:2

9. Photo caption in *La Prensa* January 12th 1978

10. AMPRONAC Managua 1978, quoted in Deighton et al 'Sweet Ramparts' 1983:41

11. Lea Guido in Randall 1981:6

12. Carlos Mejía Godoy Vivirás Monimbó

13.Lea Guido in San José, July 1996

14. AMPRONAC Managua 1978 quoted in Deighton et al 1983:42

15.See *Time* April 2nd 1984:24 and *Newsweek* April 2nd 1984:49

16. Nora Astorga interviewed in *Narahuac* Managua: Ministry of Culture 1980

17. *Newsweek* April 2nd 1984:49

18. *The New York Times* March 11th 1978:4

19. *La Prensa* between March 10th and 15th 1978: various articles on front and back pages

20. Daisy Zamora Afeites de la Muerte in 'La Mujer Nicaragüense en la Poesía':345

21. Obituary by Sofía Montenegro *Barricada* February 16th 1988

22. Nora and the Dog *Time Magazine* April 2nd 1984:24

23. Sister Rina Molina Managua December 7th 1994. Sister Rina Molina had been some years ahead of Nora at the Colegio Teresiano. She later became Principal.

24. *Time Magazine* April 2nd 1984:24

25.*The Times* February 16th 1988

Into the Mountains

1. Benjamin Zeledón, a precursor to Sandino, fought for the freedom of Nicaragua against an invasion of the US marines in 1912. With his army of 300 men he was captured and shot.

2.In the film by Deborah Schaffer and Adam Friedson, 'Fire on the Mountain', which looked at the progress and problems since the Triumph (1987)

3. Felipe Peña Son las Cinco y Media in Livingstone 1993:96-97

4. In Randall 1981:132

5. Quoted in the article by Art Harris October 4th 1984

6.See for example the photograph taken by Perry Kretz in 'Descalzos a la Victoria' Hannibal/Stern 1980

7. As described in the novel 'La Mujer Habitada' by Gioconda Belli 1988:307-08

8. Omar Cabezas 1982:95

9. Omar Cabezas 1982:246

10.In Randall 1981:125

11.Collinson (ed) 1990:116

12. Ana Julia Guido in Randall 1981:132

13. Quoted in the article by Art Harris October 4th 1984

14. In Randall 1981:125

15. Omar Cabezas 1982:123

16. Tomás Borge 1992:308

17. Omar Cabezas 1982:225

18. Rius 1982:115

19. Deighton et al 1983:42

20. Randall 1983:27-29

21. Alejandro Guevara interviewed in *Barricada* October 4th 1979: back page

22. Alejandro Guevara interviewed in Randall 1983:105-6

23. In Randall 1981:127

24. Chapter III Article 16, quoted in Tomás Borge 1992:250-51

The Triumph

1. Gioconda Belli interviewed in Randall 1994:176-77

2. Randall 1994:230

3. In Randall 1981:47

4. Pearce 1982: 125-26. It was widely understood that, from 1979, the US laundered aid to the dictatorship, and later to the Contras, through Israel.

5. Livingstone 1993:255

6. Daisy Zamora Radio Sandino in 'La Mujer Nicaragüense en la Poesía':370-82

7. In Randall 1994:243

8. Deighton et al 1983:42-43

9. Daisy Zamora Radio Sandino in 'La Mujer Nicaragüense en la Poesía':377-78

10. Amada Pineda in Randall 19981:90-91

11. Pearce 1982:126-27

12. ibid:127

13.Ruis:118

14. Daisy Zamora Radio Sandino in 'La Mujer Nicaragüense en la Poesía':376

15. ibid:382

16. In the film by Deborah Schaffer and Adam Friedson

17. Patria Libre: 19 de julio 1979 in Zamora 1992:302-03

18. In Randall 1994:211-12

19. Pearce 1982:127

20. In Randall 1981:127

21. In Randall 1994:176

22. Omar Cabezas in the film by Deborah Schaffer and Adam Friedson

23. In Randall 1981:124

24. ibid:124-25

25. In Randall 1994:54

26. Deighton et al 1982:43

27. In Randall 1994:51

28. In Randall 1994:175-77

29. Dora María was not related to Carlos Nuñez

The Tribunals

1. See *Envio* Jails and Justice in Nicaragua Vol 5 No 64 October 1986:20

2. In Randall 1981:127

3. Tomás Borge quoted in Keesings:30317

4. *Envio* Human Rights. Nicaragua's Record Vol 6 No 76 1987:24

5. *Envio* Jails and Justice in Nicaragua Vol 5 No 64 October 1986:25

6. Keesings:30317

7. In Randall 1981:116

8. ibid.

9. *Barricada* Managua January 4th 1980:5

10 *Barricada* Managua January 5th 1980:10

11. Luis Enrique Mejía Godoy La Venganza in Livingstone 1993:88-89

12. Livingstone 1993: Introduction

13. Keesings:30317

14. Sofia Montenegro in Randall 1994:295-99

15. Consuelo Romero García, Guadelupe Romero's sister, interviewed in Managua March 12th 1996

16. Amada Pineda in Randall 1981:80

17. *Barricada* January 2nd 1980:8

18. Deighton et al 1983:118-19

19. Deighton et al: 102 (from a conversation quoted in Thomas W Walker (ed) 'Nicaragua in Revolution', NW York: Praeger 1982)

20. Training manual 'Dawn of the People', reproduced in Deighton et al:103

21. Deighton et al:108

22. Livingstone 1993:5

23. *Envio* Becoming Visible. Women in Nicaragua Vol 6 No 78 1987:27

24. ibid:3

26. Patricia M Chuchryk Women in the Revolution in Walker 1991:146-47

27. In Randall 1981:91-92

28. Keesings:30592

29. United Nations World Conference of the UN Decade for Women, July 14-31 1980. Item 8, Review and Evaluation of Progress Achieved in the Implementation of the World Plan of Action: Descriptive List of National Machineries. Document 80-12792:28

30. ibid. Item 8, Review and Evaluation of Global and Regional Programmes of the UN System. Document 80-14915:20-21

31. ibid, Item 10, Review and Evaluation of Progress Achieved in the Implementation of the World Plan of Action: Political Participation and International Co-operation and the Strengthening of International Peace. Document 80-04005:12-13

32. *Envio* Jails and Justice in Nicaragua Vol 5 No 64:17

The Foreign Ministry

1. Victor Hugo Tinoco, then Secretary for the Department of International Relations of the FSLN, was interviewed in London in October 1995

2. Keesings:30317

3. See examples in Dakin M, Daniel P et al (eds) 1986

4. Harry E Vanden Foreign Policy in Walker 1991:299

5. Pearce 1982:152

6. Vanden op.cit.

7. ibid: 295

8. Gioconda Belli interviewed in Randall 1994:188-89

9. Keesings:30317

10. *Washington Post* December 28th 1980, quoted in Pearce 1982:173

11. Quoted in Art Harris October 4th 1984

12. Victor Hugo Tinoco

13. At the time of the interview Dora was National Co-ordinator of AMNLAE

14. At the time of the interview Consuelo was Executive Assistant in IXCHEN, the women's health research and development centre

15. Gloria now teaches at the Universidad Centroamericana

16. Recounted by Nemer Debas, grandson to Nora's chauffeur Carlos Orozco (now deceased) in Managua March 13th 1996

17. *Envio* Becoming Visible. Women in Nicaragua Vol 6 No 78 1987:28

18. Gioconda Belli Nicaragua Agua Fuego in Livingstone 1993:202-203

19. *Envio* Human Rights. Nicaragua's Record Vol 6 No 76 1987:24

20. Mirna Cunningham in Randall 1994:72-73

21. ibid.

22. Robelo had left the Junta the previous year and had organised demonstrations against what he called the totalitarianism of the Sandinistas. In response, crowds came out to resist the demonstrators and the MDN offices were sacked.

23. Arlen Siu was a student at León who died in combat in 1975.

24. Tomás Borge 1982. This speech from the 5th anniversary of the women's movement, León, September 29th 1982, was first printed in *Barricada,* Managua October 4th 1982.

25.William Goodfellow and James Morrell From Contadora to Esquipulas to Sapoá and Beyond in Walker 1991:371

26. Quoted in Art Harris October 4th 1984

Diplomacy

1. *The Times* March 24th 1984. The observer was Eduardo Calles, vice-president of El Salvador's Democratic Revolutionary Front.

2. See *Barricada* April 5th 1984:1

3. Tony Jenkins Ambassador may be rejected *Guardian* April 2nd 1984

5. Joan Omang US rejects Nicaragua's envoy bid *Washington Post* April 19th 1984:A1

6. *Time* April 2nd 1984:24

7. Phyllis Rose in HERS *New York Times* April 26th

8. What becomes a legend most? *Newsweek* April 2nd 1984:49

9. New Nicaraguan Ambassador to US *Associated Press* March 22nd 1984. Caption that accompanied the syndicated photograph (see front cover)

10. Interviewed in New York September 13th 1996

11. Keesings: 34141

12. Alan Riding Nicaragua warns of a move by the US *New York Times* November 15th 1984 Section A:10

13. Marc Cooper Nicaragua's new first lady *Houston Post* January 6th 1985:2D

14. Randall 'Sandino's Daughters Revisited' 1994

15. *Envio* No 83, quoted from Randall 1984

16. See article by Elaine Sciolino 1986

17. Interviewed by Dierdre Hyde and Margaret Nixon

18. *Envio* December 1987:28

19. *Envio* December 1987:24

20. As recounted by Michèle Najlis in Randall 1994:57 The interview with Dora María Téllez is from Rosalba Rolón Women in Leadership - Health in Nicaragua *MADRE Speaks* Vol 2. No1 1985:4

21. *National Review* April 5th 1985:18-19

22. Miguel d'Escoto quoted in *Barricada* February 15th 1988:5

23. Lea Guido interviewed July 17th 1996

24. Keesings:34141

25. *Envio* November 1987:28

26. *Envio* November 1987:28

211

27. Elaine Sciolino US and Nicaragua clash as UN opens discussion of region *The New York Times* November 13th 1885

28. The Lima Group had been set up in August 1985 to support the Contadora Group. It consisted of Argentina, Peru, Brazil and Uruguay.

29. United Nations Security Council Official Records 40th Session Supplement for October, November and December 1985. Document S/17675 Letter from Victor Hugo Tinoco

30. Keesings Vol XXXII: 34511

31. ibid.

The United Nations

1. Rosalba Rolón Women in Leadership - Health in Nicaragua *MADRE Speaks* Vol 2. No1 1985:6

2. Quoted in Mary Anne Weaver The femme fatale of Sandinista diplomacy *The Christian Science Monitor* August 15th 1986 International Section:9

3. Sciolino *New York Times Magazine* September 28th 1986

4. *The Nation* Editorial March 29th 1986

5. According to Sciolino, op.cit.

6. Lea Guido July 17th 1996

7. Miriam Hooker Pearl Lagoon November 30th 1995

8. See Pathfinder Press 1985:xviii

9. Lea Guido, op.cit.

10. Kevin M Cahill interviewed in New York September 16th 1996

11. Keesings Vol XXXII:34548

12. ibid.

13. ibid.

14. See United Nations Report of the International Court of Justice. August 1st 1985-July 31st 1986:4-12

15. Quoted in *Envio* November 1987:39

16. United National Security Council Supplement for April, May and June 1986, Document S/18187

17. United Nations Security Council Records , Document S/PV.2695

18. Security Council Records, Document S/PV2696:70-71

19. Security Council Records, Document S/PV.2698:29-30

20. Real de Azua in *Barricada* February 17th 1988:1221.

21. Sciolino 1986:28-29

22. Real de Azua 1988:12

23. Sciolino, op. cit.

24. Weaver, op.cit.

Tensions

1. Keesings: 31565A; 31113A; 33205

2. Mary Anne Weaver <u>The femme fatale of Sandinista diplomacy</u> *The Christian Science Monitor* August 15th 1986 International Section:9

3. Vernon Walters in Security Council Records, Document S/PV.2701:3

4. ibid:3-4

5.Jacqueline Sharkey <u>Back in Control</u> *Common Cause Magazine* September/October 1986. Quoted in Angharad Valdivia <u>US Intervention in Nicaraguan Media</u> in Walker 1991:355-56

6. Vernon Walters in Security Council Records, Document S/PV.2701:17

7. Vernon Walters in Security Council Records, Document S/PV.2701:42

8. Real de Azua 1988:12

9. Sofía Montenegro's obituary of Nora 1988

10. Sciolino's article 1986

11. Vanden <u>Foreign Policy</u> in Walker 1991:303

12. Jennifer Uglow 'The Macmillan's Dictionary of Women's Biography' 1989

13. Grethel Vargas interviewed in New York September 23rd 1996

14. United Nations Document A/42/PV.100

15. Real de Azua 1988:12

16. Sciolino 1986

17. Real de Azua 1988

18. Kathryn Cahill <u>Nicaragua's Secret Weapon</u> New York October 1987, unpublished article

19. Safiya Henderson Holms the night I saw nora astorga sigh published in *MADRE Speaks* Spring 1988:18

20. Keesings: 33205

21. *Envio* November 1986:14

22. ibid.

23. Quoted in news item UPI *Washington News* December 11th 1986

24. Keesings: 35115

25. Keesings: 354339

26. Keesings:35439

27. *Envio* February 1987:8-9

28. Vanden Foreign Policy in Walker 1991

The Struggle Continues

1. FSLN 'Women and the Sandinista Revolution' Managua 1987:39

2. Sofia Montenegro Feminismo, Poder y Democracia - la experiencia de Nicaragua Managua AMNLAE October 1987

3. Susan Meiselas New York November 21st 1996

4. Interviewed in New York September 23rd 1996

5. Don Casey interviewed in New York September 13th 1996

6. Sciolino 1986

7. Kathryn Cahill Nicaragua's Secret Weapon New York October 1987, unpublished article

8. Wolfgang Saxon Nora Astorga, a Sandinista Hero and Delegate to the UN, Dies at 39 *New York Times* February 15th 1988:A18

10. Kathryn Cahill, op. cit.

11. *Barricada* July 12th 1987:1-2

12. *Barricada* July 18th 1987:2; July 19th 1987:3; July 20th 1987:3

13. Daisy Zamora Afeites de la Muerte in Zamora 1992:345-46

14. Nora Astorga in her own words (Introduction): 40

15. United Nations General Assembly 41st Session Provisional Verbatim Report A/41/PV.63:29

16. United Nations General Assembly Official Records of the 42nd Session Supplement No.24 (A/42/24) Report of the UN Council for Namibia:21

17. UN General Assembly A/41/PV.63:27

18. Memory by Trevor Nunn, incorporating lines from TS Elliot's Rhapsody on a Windy Night in the show Cats

19. Grethel Vargas September 24th 1996. The final quote is from a fax written by Grethel and sent to AMNLAE by women of the Nicaraguan mission, to be read out on International Women's Day March 3rd 1988

20. Washington September 19th 1996

21. Mary Anne Weaver The femme fatale of Sandinista diplomacy *The Christian Science Monitor* August 15th 1986 International Section:9

22. Mr Belonogov representing the USSR, UN General Assembly Doc. A/42/PV.100:8-10

23. Kathryn Cahill Nicaragua's Secret Weapon New York October 1987, unpublished article

24. Vanden Foreign Policy in Walker 1991

The Final Exile

1. Susan Meiselas New York September 14th 1996

2. Miguel d'Escoto quoted in *Barricada* February 15th 1988:5

3. Kathy Engel Nora's Song, written on Martin Luther King's birthday January 18th 1988, published in *MADRE Speaks* Spring 1988:17

4. Kevin Cahill New York September 16th 1996

5. ibid.

6. Miguel d'Escoto, op.cit.

7. These three comments are by a former teacher of Nora's, who gave her great support at this time.

8. Sister Rina Molina Managua December 6th 1994

9. Linda Rodriguez-Flores in *MADRE Speaks* Spring 1988:34

10. William Goodfellow and James Morrell From Contadora to Esquipulas to Sapoá and Beyond in Walker 1991:382-83

11. *Barricada* February 14th 1988:1

12. *Barricada* February 15th 1988:1

13. Hermana, compañera y heroína de la paz *Barricada* February 15th 1988:5

14. Gloria Tünnermann Managua March 10th 1996

15. Misa Campesina translated by Dinah Livingstone as Nicaraguan Mass London: Catholic Institute for International Relations 1986; reissued by Nicaragua Solidarity Campaign 1996

16. Quoted in Nora Astorga in her own words: 40

17. Solemnidad y conmoción en funerales de Nora Astorga *Barricada* February 16th 1988:5

18. Grethel Vargas, fax from the Nicaraguan mission to the UN. March 3rd 1988

19. Real de Azua 1988

20. United Nations Security Council 2791st Meeting Doc. S/PV.2791 February 16th 1988:2

21. Hugh Scotland A Poem to the Pre-Eminent Sandinista Heroine Room 491, UN Secretarial Building, New York February 16th 1988

22. MADRE In Memoriam: The Honorable Nora Astorga *The New York Times* February 19th 1988

Epilogue

1.UN General Assembly 42nd Session February 29th 1988 Doc. A/42/PV.100:1-27

2.Mimeo, copy obtained from Grethel Vargas

3. Kevin M Cahill MD A Bridge to Peace New York: Haymarket Doyma 1988

4. Lea Guido San José July 21st 1996

216

Bibliography

Belli, Gioconda (1988) *La Mujer Habitada*. Managua, Vanguardia

Borge, Tomás (1983) *La mujer y la revolución nicaragüense*. New York, Pathfinder Press (intro. Margaret Yayko)

Borge, Tomás (1992) *The Patient Impatience: from boyhood to guerrilla*. New York, Curbstone Press (trans. R Bartley, D Flakell and S Yoneda)

Brenes, Ada Julia, Lovo Ivania and Saakes Silvia (1991*) La mujer nicaragüense en los años 80*. Managua, Ediciones Nicarao

Cabezas, Omar (1982) *La montaña es algo más que una inmensa estepa verde*. Managua, Editorial Nueva Nicaragua

Collinson, Helen (ed) (1990) *Women and Revolution in Nicaragua*. London, Zed Books

Daniel, Patricia and Parri, Llinos Non (1994) *Adlais o America Ladin / Voices from Latin America* Bangor, Môn and Arfon Central America Group / Christian Aid

Dakin, Mary, Daniel, Pat et al (eds) (1986) *Nicaragua: 4th Battle of the Coffee Harvest*. London, Nicaragua Solidarity Campaign/ War on Want

Deighton, Jane et al. (1983) *Sweet Ramparts. Women in Revolutionary Nicaragua*. London, War on Want/ Nicaragua Solidarity Campaign

Envio Managua, Instituto Historico Centroamericano

> Vol 5 No 64 'Jails and Justice in Nicaragua' Oct 86: 14 -28
>
> Vol 5 No 65 'Hasenfus: Nothing but the Facts' Nov 1986: 3 -19
>
> Vol 5 No 66 'Trail of Illegality Ends at Contragate' Dec 1986: 3-19
>
> Vol 6 No 67 'The Contragate Board Game' February 1987: 2-11
>
> Vol 6 No 76 'Human Rights. Nicaragua's Record' Oct 1987: 17-39
>
> Vol 6 No 77 'Church-State Relations. Part I' Nov 1987: 25-42
>
> Vol 6 No 78 'Becoming Visible. Women in Nicaragua' Dec 1987: 17-31
>
> Vol 7 No 82 'Nora Astorga in her own words' April 1988: 40-55
>
> Vol 7 No 83 'Women, Poetry, New Nicaraguan Culture' May 1988: 15-33

FSLN National Directorate (1987) *Women and the Sandinista Revolution.* Managua, Editorial Vanguardia

Harris, Art (1984) 'The Sandinistas' Sister-in-Arms: The Ardor of a Revolutionary' *The Washington Post* October 4th 1984: B1

Livingstone Dinah (trans) (1993) *Poets of the Nicaraguan Revolution* London, Katabasis

Montenegro, Sofía (1988) 'Nora, guerrillera de la paz y la vida' *Barricada* February 16, 1988: 3

Ortega, Humberto Saavedra (1980) *50 años de lucha Sandinista.* Habana: Editorial de Ciencias Sociales

Pathfinder Press (1985) *Nicaragua The Sandinista People's Revolution. Speeches by Sandinista leaders.* New York, Pathfinder Press

Pearce, Jenny (1982) *Under the Eagle. US Intervention in Central America and the Caribbean.* London, Latin American Bureau

Randall, Margaret (1981) *Sandino's Daughters: Testimonies of Women in Struggle.* Vancouver BC, New Star Books

Randall, Margaret (1983) *Christians in the Nicaraguan Revolution.* Vancouver BC, New Star Books

Randall, Margaret (1984) *Risking a Somersault in the Air - Conversations with Nicaraguan Writers.* San Francisco, Solidarity Publications

Randall, Margaret (1994) *Sandino's Daughters Revisited. Feminism in Nicaragua.* New Brunswick NJ, Rutgers University Press

Real de Azua, Santiago (1988) 'ONU rinde homenaje a Nora Astorga' B*arricada* February 17 1988: 12

Rius (Eduardo del Río) (1984) *Nicaragua for Beginners* London / New York, Writers and Readers

Schaffer, Deborah and Adam Friedson (1987) *Fire on the Mountain* (in association with Common Sense Foundation)

Sciolino, Elaine (1986) 'Nicaragua's UN Voice' *The New York Times Magazine* September 28 1986: 29

Selser, Gregorio (1966) *Sandino, General de Hombres Libres* Costa Rica, Editorial Universitaria Centroamericana (2nd edition)

218

Walker, Thomas (ed) (1991) *Revolution and Counterrevolution in Nicaragua.* Boulder, Colorado, West View Press

Zamora, Daisy (1992) *La Mujer Nicaragüense en la Poesía. Antologia.* Managua, Nueva Nicaragua

Glossary of Nicaraguan Women

Báez Gladys, fought on the western front against Somoza, then member of the National Assembly, also former General Secretary of AMNLAE

Belli Gioconda, FSLN militant, poet and novelist

Campos Gloria, former member of the National Assembly

Carrión Gloria, founder member of AMPRONAC, sister to Luis Carrión

Chamorro Violeta Barrios de, owns *La Prensa*, was married to Pedro Joaquín Chamorro, then a member of the Junta of National Reconstruction, more recently President leading a right wing coalition government

Chow Marlene, student activist in León with Jorgé Jenkins

Clarke Rita, worked at the Nicaraguan Embassy in Washington, now runs the US-Nicaragua Friendship Association, is sister to Miguel d'Escoto

Cunningham Mirna, FSLN militant, doctor, former deputy in the National Assembly and member of the Regional Autonomous Council of the Northern Atlantic Coast

Espinosa Luisa Amanda, first woman martyr of the revolution, after whom the women's organisation, AMNLAE, was named

Gabuardi Gloria, FSLN militant, poet, studied Law with Nora

Guido Ana Julia, led the rearguard coming in from Honduras in the last weeks before the Triumph, then was bodyguard in the Ministry of the Interior

Guido Lea, former Minister of Social Welfare, General Secrtary of AMNLAE, now works in the Pan American Health Organisation

Herrera Leticia, FSLN militant known as Vicky, former Deputy President of the National Assembly

Hooker Miriam, runs the Centre for Human Rights in Bluefield, previously worked at the Nicaraguan Embassy in Washington and Harare

Molina Rina (Sister), former student and then Principal at the Colegio Teresiano

Montenegro Sofía, FSLN militant, journalist and feminist

Morales Marisol, lawyer to the National Assembly, attended Colegio Teresiano and UCA with Nora

Murillo Rosario, poet, former Secretary General of the Sandinista Association of Cultural Workers, attended Colegio Teresiano with Nora

Najlis María Cristina, Nora's best friend at school

Najlis Michèle, poet and journalist, now Director of Cultural Affairs at UCA, María Cristina's older cousin

Randall Margaret, poet, journalist, teacher and photographer, who has recorded many aspects of the Nicaraguan revolution - an honorary Nicaraguan! now lives in New Mexico

Romero García Consuelo, Guadelupe's sister, worked with Nora in the Foreign Ministry, now at IXCHEN

Romero Guadelupe, Nora's personal assistant during the Tribunals and at the Foreign Ministry, now works in El Salvador

Pereira Rosa, married to Carlos Tünnermann

Salinas Guadelupe, lawyer, childhood friend, attended UCA with Nora, now works in the Centre for Constitutional Rights

Siu Arlen, FSLN militant, poet and singer, died fighting in 1975

Téllez Dora María, *comandante*, led the raid on the National Palace in 1978, formerly Minister of Health and deputy in the National Assembly

Tijerino Doris María, FSLN leader, *comandante*, former President of AMNLAE, Chief of Police and still a deputy in the National Assembly

Tünnermann Gloria, worked at the Foreign Ministry, now at the UCA

Vargas Grethel, diplomat at the Nicaraguan Mission to the UN, also attended Colegio Teresiano with Nora and worked at the Foreign Ministry

Vargas Milú, FSLN militant, lawyer, runs the Carlos Nuñez Téllez Centre for Constitutional Rights

Zamora Daisy, FSLN militant, poet, former Deputy Minister of Culture, attended Colegio Teresiano and UCA with Nora

Zeledón Dora, formerly at the Foreign Ministry, recently General Secretary of AMNLAE, now a deputy in the National Assembly

Glossary of Nicaraguan Men

Agüero Carlos, law student at the UCA with Nora, fought in the mountains and died in combat

Alvarado José María, FSLN leader before 1979, Nora's second partner

Arce Bayardo, fellow student of Nora's, later member of the FSLN National Directorate and deputy in the National Assembly

Borge Tomás, the only surviving founder member of the FSLN, former member of the National Directorate and Minister of the Interior

Buitrago Julio, founder member of the FSLN, killed in combat in 1969

Cabezas Omar, student activist and *guerrillero*, deputy in the National Assembly

Cardenal Ernesto, priest, poet, former Minister of Culture

Cardenal Fernando, priest, teacher at the UCA, former Minister for Education, brother to Ernesto

Carrión Luis, former member of FSLN National Directorate and Deputy-Minister of the Interior

Chamorro Pedro Joaquín, editor of *La Prensa*, assassinated in 1978, married to Violeta

Chamorro Xavier, editor of *El Nuveo Diario*, brother to Pedro Joaquín

Cruz Arturo, member of the Junta for National Reconstruction, then Nicaraguan Ambassador to the US, left the revolution and became a member of the Contra directorate

Cuadra Joaquín, student at the UCA, involved in the grassroots Christian community movement

d'Escoto Miguel, former priest, member of The Twelve, then Foreign Minister

Escobar José Benito, FSLN leader died in action before 1979

Fonseca Amador Carlos, one of the founders of the FSLN, died fighting in 1976

García Alfonso, member of the FER, fellow student of Nora's at the UCA

Godoy Carlos Mejía and Godoy Luis Enrique Mejía, brothers and suspensionians, whose songs were an inspiration to the people during the revolutionary struggle

Guevara Alejandro, member of Ernesto Cardenal's community on Solentiname, then one of the chiefs of staff who fought on the Southern Front

Hassan Moisés, member of the Junta of National Reconstruction

Jenkins Molieri Jorgé, student activist, Nora's first husband, Nicaraguan Ambassador to Sweden and Brazil, now works for World Health Organisation

Laviana Gaspar García, Spanish priest who fought with Nora on the Southern Front, died in action in 1979

Molina Uriel, priest, taught at the UCA and helped to found the grassroots Christian communities

Morales Avilés Ricardo, FSLN leader, academic (at the UCA) and poet, killed in action in 1973

Navarro Jorgé, founder member of the FSLN, killed in combat in 1963

Pastora Eden, led the National Palace raid in 1978, left the revolution in 1982 and set up the ARDE Contra force

Ortega Camilo, FSLN leader, died in action in 1978

Ortega Daniel, brother to Camilo, former President of Nicaragua, member of the FSLN National Directorate and Secretary General of the FSLN

Ortega Humberto, brother to Daniel, former head of the Sandinista Armed Forces and member of the FSLN National Directorate

Peña Felipe, poet who fought on the Southern Front, died in action before the Triumph in 1979

Pomares Germán, FSLN leader, died in action before the Triumph in 1979

Ramírez Sergio, writer, former member of the Twelve, the Junta and then Deputy President, former deputy in the National Assembly

Robelo Alfonso, former banker and member of the Junta for National Reconstruction, before leaving to support the counter-revolution

Rugama Leonel, former priest, poet, killed in action in 1970

Ruiz Henri, former Minister of Foreign Co-operation and member of the FSLN Directorate

Sánchez Hilario, led the Christmas Party raid in 1974 as well as Operation *El Perro* in 1978

Sotelo Casimiri, student at the UCA, captured and assassinated in 1967

Tinoco Victor Hugo, former Deputy Minister in the Foreign Ministry, then Head of International Relations for the FSLN, now deputy in the National Assembly

Tünnermann Carlos, former Rector of the National University in León, then Nicaraguan Ambassador to the US

Turcios Oscar, FSLN leader, killed in action 1973

Wheelock Jaime, former member of the FSLN National Directorate, former Minister of Agriculture

Zeledón Benjamin, led resistance to 1912 invasion of Nicaragua by US Marines

Glossary of Organisations

AMNLAE   *Asociación de Mujeres Nicaragüenses 'Luisa Amanda Espinosa'*: women's association set up in 1979 and named after the first Sandinista woman who died in combat

AMPRONAC   *Asociación de Mujeres Ante de la Problematica Nacional*: women's association confronting the national problem (the problem being the dictator Somoza) set up in 1977

ARDE   *Alianza Revolucionaria Democratica*: counter-revolutionary group operating out of Costa Rica from 1983, led by Eden Pastora

Los Doce   The Group of Twelve: group of prominent Nicaraguans who formed in 1977 in support of the FSLN, included priests, literary figures, businessmen

FAO   *Frente de Alianza en Opposición*: Broad Opposition Front which formed before 1979 against Somoza

FDN   *Fuerzas Democraticas Nicaragüenses*: the name of the counterrevolutionary forces operating from near the Honduran border, consisted mainly of former National Guardsmen, started in 1981

FER   *Frente Estudiantil Revolucionaria* : the student arm of the FSLN

FSLN   *Frente Sandinista de Liberación Nacional*: the Sandinista National Liberation Front, now a political party

MISURASATA Alliance of Miskitos, Sumos, Ramas and Sandinistas, which began to collaborate with the Contra in the early 1980s and was later dissolved

Contadora Group Latin American initiative composed of the foreign ministers of Colombia, Mexico, Panama and Venezuela, with the stated purpose to negotiate a peaceful solution to the Central American conflict; named after the Panamanian island where the group first met

Arias Peace Plan Central American Peace Plan named after the then President of Costa Rica, developed in 1987 to replace Contadora

Patricia Daniel
teacher and writer in education and women's issues, worked in Nicaragua
during the 1980s, lives in North Wales with her family, promotes language
rights and equal representation for women.

CAM
promotes teaching and research for and about women across the world.